THE OBAMA MENU

DINING WITH BARACK OBAMA

TCB CAFE
Publishing & Media

TasteTV

EDITOR IN CHIEF: A.K. CRUMP

PHOTOGRAPHY: CREDIT AND THANKS GOES TO ALL ACKNOWLEDGED PHOTOGRAPHERS, INCLUDING RESTAURANTS AND OTHER COMPANIES FEATURED HEREIN, AS WELL AS TO ALL ORGANIZATIONS AND INDIVIDUALS THAT CONTRIBUTED PHOTOGRAPHS TO THIS PUBLICATION, INCLUDING BILL EYSTER, TIM KELLEY, AND "CLIFF"

FRONT COVER IMAGES: TIM KELLEY, WHITE HOUSE PHOTOGRAPHY
BACK COVER: THE KAHALA RESORT

SPECIAL THANKS TO THE CRUMP FAMILY, GEORGIA PETERSON DE MACHUCA, THE LATE ROBERT GREEN. THING 1 AND THING 2, AND TasteTV AND THE INTERNATIONAL CHOCOLATE SALON.

The Obama Menu

First Edition

 **tcb-cafe** Publishing and media
PO Box 471706
SAN FRANCISCO, CALIFORNIA 94147
WWW.CAFEANDRE.COM, WWW.TASTETV.COM
USA

COPYRIGHT © 2009,
TCB-CAFE PUBLISHING AND MEDIA, /TASTETV

•ISBN-10: 0979864070
•ISBN-13: 978-0979864070

NOTE ABOUT RECIPES: THE RECIPES IN THIS GUIDE ARE "AS IS." IN OTHER WORDS, WE DON'T TINKER WITH WHAT THE CHEFS OR MIXOLOGISTS HAVE GIVEN TO US FOR THE GUIDE. IF YOU HAVE A QUESTION ABOUT A PARTICULAR RECIPE, THIS GIVES YOU A GOOD EXCUSE FOR CONTACTING ITS CREATOR IN PERSON.

THE OBAMA MENU

DINING WITH BARACK OBAMA

THE OBAMA MENU
2001-2007

Political Appetizers and Sound Bites

HINTS OF A
MASTER RECIPE

Chicago, Illinois

Barack Obama begins his public career in eating food in front of a television audience by appearing on the program Check Please! in Chicago. Unfortunately, rumor has it that he was so good they decided not to run the episode until he ran for President.

In the episode, Barack explains why he recommended Southern-style restaurant Dixie Kitchen and Bait Shop to his fellow diners and television audience:

> BARACK: "That is one of the things that I like about this place, the prices are right and the portions are good...It's done booming business.. It represents the kind of neighborhood restaurant that every neighborhood should have. People feel comfortable there, they take their families there."

> BARACK: "It's not gourmet cuisine, but that's not why I go to Dixie Kitchen. I'm not looking for some fancy presentation, with extraordinarily subtle flavors. I'm looking for food that tastes good at a good price."

The Obama Menu begins

"What if it was as easy to get a book as it
is to rent a DVD or pick up McDonald's? What
if instead of a toy in every Happy Meal, there
was a book? What if there were portable libraries
that rolled through parks and playgrounds like ice
cream trucks?"

Barack Obama
June 27th
Speech to the American Library Association

New York, New York

Barack begins the traditional process of fundraising: private dinner and cocktail parties with wealthy and influential supporters.

Obama goes to four fundraising parties in New York. Two of the parties were hosted by former investment banker Robert Wolf, one by Edgar Bronfman Jr, and one by music mogul Antonio LA Reid. According to New York Magazine, Obama supporters were excited about their success, stating that,

> "We had Beyoncé and Patricia Duff, Jay-Z and Jamie Rubin, Jermaine Dupri and Jonathan Soros. We raised north of $350,000 in two hours. And that's when it became crystal clear to all of us: We can raise this money."

Beyonce'

Sunday
November 11
Des Moines, Iowa

Iowa Jefferson Jackson Dinner

Barack Obama:

"A little less than one year from today, you will go into the voting booth and you will select the President of the United States of America. Now, here's the good news -- the name George W. Bush will not be on the ballot. The name of my cousin Dick Cheney will not be on the ballot. We've been trying to hide that for a long time. Everybody has a black sheep in the family. The era of Scooter Libby justice, and Brownie incompetence, and Karl Rove politics will finally be over.

But the question you're going to have to ask yourself when you caucus in January and you vote in November is, "What's next for America?" We are in a defining moment in our history. Our nation is at war. The planet is in peril. The dream that so many generations fought for feels as if it's slowly slipping away. We are working harder for less. We've never paid more for health care or for college. It's harder to save and it's harder to retire. And most of all we've lost faith that our leaders can or will do anything about it..."

"Our moment is now.

I don't want to spend the next year or the next four years re-fighting the same fights that we had in the 1990s.

I don't want to pit Red America against Blue America, I want to be the President of the United States of America."

THE 2008 PRESIDENTIAL CAMPAIGN YEAR OFFICIALLY BEGINS

The Main Course

THE OBAMA TEAM EATS ITS WAY ACROSS AMERICA

Richmond, Virginia

Photographer and Correspondent, Tim Kelley : "These pictures were taken on 2/9/2008. I was asked to take pictures at the Jefferson Jackson dinner, where the keynote speakers were presidential hopefuls Hillary Clinton and Barack Obama. I actually had little time to eat in the excitement of the evening and only managed to scarf down some salad and a few dinner rolls!"

Scranton, Pennsylvania

"Waffle-gate"

Obama declares to over inquisitive reporters,"'Why can't I just eat my waffle?"

At a diner in Scranton, candidate Obama stopped for a breakfast of sausages, orange juice, and waffles. Though recently he has given local reporters access for interviews, the national press corps has not had any for several days. When one reporters asks for his reaction to President Jimmy Carter's statements about a positive meeting with Palestinian faction Hamas, Obama replies,

"Why can't I just eat my waffle?"

The Republican National Committee then sends an email to the press stating that,

"Today, Obama continued to dodge questions from the media, responding that he just wanted to eat his waffle."

MAY

Fort Wayne, Indiana

Obama Menu Lesson: *If coming to support your candidate at a public park, expect to celebrate it with a lot of food...*

"*These photos were taken at a rally in Fort Wayne, Indiana in early May on the Sunday right before the Indiana primaries (2008). The rally was at Headwaters Park, and there were around 4 or 5 thousand people there.*"
- Bill Eyster, Flickr: Willie_57

The size of the crowd, as well as the presence of so much food, was somewhat unexpected.

MAY

Fort Wayne, Indiana

Photos by Bill Eyster,
Flickr: Willie_57

Fort Wayne, Indiana

MAY

Fort Wayne, Indiana

Photos by Bill Eyster,
Flickr: Willie_57

Sunday
June 1
Sioux Falls, South Dakota

Obama Menu Lesson: *Pancakes are safer to eat in front of reporters than waffles.*

Obama attends a pancake breakfast with veterans and military families at the Lyon Fairgrounds. National reports are that Obama catches a flipped pancake."

Obama says during the brunch,

> "John McCain -- like George Bush -- opposed it, even though John McCain didn't come back to vote, " Obama explained, "I don't understand why he would side with George Bush in opposing a bipartisan bill that does so much to make college affordable for veterans. George Bush and John McCain may think that the bill is too generous, but I could not disagree more."

Reports ABC News:

> Obama ended his visit with veterans, eating a pancake brunch -- the pancake chef tossed three flapjacks high in the air and Obama caught them on a plate.

Adds Mark Halperin of TIME Magazine and blog, The Page:

> With an echo of Obama's famous "Why can't I just eat my waffle?" line, the Land of Lincolner chats with The Page:
>
> Obama: You guys having some?
>
> TIME: Can't we just eat our pancakes?
>
> Obama: You can.
>
> TIME: That's a little joke.
>
> Obama: There you go.

Wednesday
June 4
United States of America

Obama responds to a question by San Antonio Current reporter Ari Levaux about what he would bring to a potluck with what he calls his family chili recipe.

Says candidate Obama:

> "I've been using this chili recipe since college and would bring it to any potluck. I can't reveal all the secrets, but if you make it right, it's just got the right amount of bite, the right amount of oomph in it, and it will clear your sinuses."

Obama Family Chili Recipe

INGREDIENTS
1 large onion, chopped
1 green pepper, chopped
Several cloves of garlic, chopped
1 Tablespoon olive oil
1 pound ground turkey or beef
1/4 teaspoon ground cumin
1/4 teaspoon ground oregano
1/4 teaspoon ground turmeric
1/4 teaspoon ground basil
1 Tablespoon chili powder
3 Tablespoon red-wine vinegar
Several tomatoes, depending on size, chopped
1 can red kidney beans

Saute onions, green pepper, and garlic in olive oil until soft. Add ground meat and brown. Combine spices together into a mixture, then add to ground meat. Add red-wine vinegar. Add tomatoes and let simmer until the tomatoes cook down. Add kidney beans and cook for a few more minutes.

Serve over white or brown rice. Garnish with grated cheddar cheese, onions, and sour cream.

Obama also begins to outline some elements of his evolving national food policy, and in particular the role of small organic farmers in or near urban centers.

Obama: "I am very familiar with the great work of … community-supported farms. These types of farms can provide an important source of fresh fruits and vegetables to inner-city communities that do not have easy access to grocery stores that sell organic foods. Moreover, farms like [these] that sell directly to consumers cut out all of the middlemen and get full retail price for their food, which increases the financial viability of small family farms."

"As president, I would implement USDA policies that promote local and regional food systems, including assisting states to develop programs aimed at community-supported farms. I also support a national farm-to-school program and am pleased that the Farm Bill provides more than $1 billion to expand healthy snacks in our schools. "

Wednesday
June 4
New York, New York

Fundraiser at the home of Bonnie and Richard Reiss
Attendees include Caroline Kennedy, Sarah Jessica Parker and Ted Sorensen.

Obama:

> "Ultimately, I'm not interested in symbolic victories. I'm interesting in actually getting work done."

Coverage of this evening's events was a game-changer not only because Obama was close to having won the Democratic Presidential nomination, but also because it began real public access to his fundraising dinners and receptions.

Says Lynn Sweet of the Chicago Sun-Times,

> "Until Obama changed his policy on Tuesday, events like these were closed [to reporters]."

The evening also signals the beginning of Obama's shift of his fundraising from an emphasis on a recording-breaking number of small Internet donations towards a balance that includes more traditional political fundraising with well-heeled and influential supporters.

Recounts Jeff Zeleny of the New York Times:

> Senator Barack Obama attended back-to-back fund-raisers Wednesday night in Manhattan — raising more than $2.5 million for the party — as a burst of new contributors turned out one day after he won enough delegates to claim the Democratic presidential nomination.

JUNE

As he stepped out of his motorcade in a light drizzle, Mr. Obama was asked how he felt now that Senator Hillary Rodham Clinton had decided to offer her endorsement of his candidacy on Saturday in Washington.

"Truth is, I haven't had time to think about it," Mr. Obama told a reporter. "This weekend, I'm going home, talk it over with Michele and we're going on a date."

Mr. Obama began the evening at the Park Avenue home of Bonnie and Richard Reiss, where 200 people paid $2,300 each for what he called "our first post-nomination event." As he uttered those words, the crowd erupted in applause, whistles and catcalls, exuberant at the notion that the campaign had drawn to a close.

Charlie Hurt of the New York Post wrote that

"as people milled around with cocktails, there was a sense of wonderment and excitement that it really was finally over. 'This primary process took a very long time,' Obama said, referring to those mythical babies who are now walking and talking. As he spoke for about 25 minutes, a dispatch from Politico's Mike Allen came across confirming ABC's report that Clinton would get out Friday.

Wednesday
June 4
New York, New York

Fundraising dinner at the Park Avenue home of Jane Hartley and Ralph Schlosstein for the the White House Victory Fund, with proceeds going to the eventual Democratic nominee.

$28,500/person, with approximately 100 people for dinner

Monday
June 9
St. Louis, Missouri

Fundraiser at the Renaissance Grand Hotel
800-Washington Avenue, 63101
$500 to $2,300/person

As Obama's candidacy gains momentum, the question of his relationship to food, and his potential national policy on food, increases.

Says the Huffington Post,

> "The Obama fundraiser tonight is putting the Republicans on notice that Missouri state Democrats are keeping the 'mo' going for Obama, not only by raising money to keep the deep organizational effort humming along -- that began months ago while the Republican nominee was napping -- but pulling together the enormous jingle-jangle for party coffers by throwing a swank VIP reception."

JUNE

*Missourians apparently did not require food along with their attendance.
Reports are that there was an open bar but only hors d'oeuvres &
cheese served. However, Lynn Sweet of the Chicago Sun-Times points
out that Obama did talk about food policy at the event in response
to the question,*

"What would an Obama administration do about the global food crisis?"

Obama answered, "Well there a lot of factors involved right
now. One of the things I want to do is make sure that
we're dealing with climate change in a meaningful way, because
changing weather patterns are the likely cause of some of the
problems that we're having, for example, in Australia, with the
drought. And those problems could get worse. Every degree of
temperature that -- every degree that the global temperature
goes up, we see 10% reductions in rice production, and so
we could have some long-term problems, and that's why I've
proposed a cap-and-trade system that will start aggressively
dealing with global warming. The second thing that we need to
do is we've got to, I think, examine our food policies to
figure out, how can we encourage increased production in poor
countries that are having the biggest problems with potential
hunger. You know, traditionally, our foreign aid is designed so
that we grow food here and then we export it there. We have
to, I think, start thinking about, can we buy some of the food
there for distribution in that country to encourage increased
production, and to give farmers in those countries more of
an incentive to grow, and then we've obviously got to provide
technical assistance so we're increasing their production more
effectively. I think that we've got to stockpile food reserves
at a global level more effectively than we have in the past.
Those stockpiles have shrunk considerably. And finally, we're
going to have to deal with increasing energy costs, which
are having an impact on overall food production and cost. So
this is going to be long challenge, and is something that
an Obama administration is going to monitor closely and take
aggressive action."

Thursday
June 12
Chicago, Illinois

Fundraising "Special Reception" at the home of Sara and James Hall for the Democratic White House Victory Fund
$28,500/person

Thursday
June 12, 2008
Chicago, Illinois

Fundraiser at the home of Leah Missbach Day and F.K. Day for "Obama for America"
$2,300/person

JUNE

Friday
June 13
Philadelphia, PA

Fundraiser cocktail reception at the Sheraton Center City Hotel
$1000-$2300/person

Obama Menu Lesson: *Cheese steaks and pancakes become a recurring theme for the Obama campaign.*

At the Sheraton Center City reception, Gov. Rendell presents Obama with a lifetime gift certificate to Pat's Steaks.

"A cheese steak once a day, and I'll have the pleasure of looking like Ed Rendell," jokes Obama.

Fortunately, campaigning is one way to work off the extra pounds, as Obama adds about Rendell, "He's got me barnstorming around the Philadelphia area tomorrow. He's wearing me out."

Attendees at the Sheraton included Sen. Bob Casey, U.S. Rep Chaka Fattah, U.S. Rep Allyson Schwartz, and musician Jon Bon Jovi, who also played "Living on a Prayer."

Reports are that attendees munched on appetizers, not Philly cheese steaks.

Friday
June 13
Philadelphia, PA

During a television interview late-night talk show host Jimmy Kimmel, over satellite, asked Obama about Father's Day:

Kimmell: "Happy Fathers Day. What's a typical Father's Day at the Obama house?"

Obama: "We usually have some experiment with waffles or pancakes and there's a lot of cleanup afterwards…They come with stuff we wouldn't normally put on pancakes like whipped cream…. Then we go to church."

Kimmel: "Are you required to report gifts as a public servant?"

Obama: "Only of it's over $50 but my children are pretty stingy…"

On Jimmy Kimmel's talk show, Obama proves once again that pancakes are always a safe topic for a politician to discuss with the media.

Monday
June 16
Detroit, Michigan

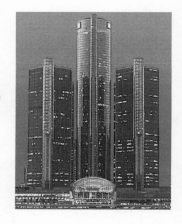

Fundraiser at the Marriott at the Renaissance Center

Al Gore provides an introduction.

Tuesday
June 17
New York, New York

Vogue & Calvin Klein host a cocktail party & Victory Fund dinner for Michelle Obama

Reports Jim Shi of Fashion Week Daily:

> Organized by Vogue's Anna Wintour and André Leon Talley, as well as Shelby Bryan and Calvin Klein, the sold-out affair afforded attendees the opportunity to contribute anywhere from $1,000 (as an attendee) to $10,000 (for a Democratic White House Victory Fund dinner at Klein's West Village home afterward). At the festive cocktail reception, guests did their part to wear their support on their sleeves--literally. Lauren Santo Domingo affixed a specially made Obama pin to her floral Oscar de la Renta dress and clutch, while Zac Posen sported a "Yes We Can, Obama 08" T-shirt underneath his blazer.
>
> After Talley, who sported another signature turban, introduced his friend Michelle, he promptly scooted off stage-- inadvertently taking the mic with him. "André, I need the mic," Obama said, gesturing with her hands.

JUNE

Isaac Mizrahi

Following an upstairs meet and greet, where she posed for photos with supporters (only water and wine were served), Mrs. Obama went downstairs.

Per Fashion Week Daily, dinner guests included Iman, Tonya Lewis Lee and Spike Lee, Isaac Mizrahi, André Balazs, Harvey Weinstein, LL Cool J, Nicole Miller and LeBron James.

Reports Shi:

> Guests sat with platefuls of food on their laps as they listened to Obama speak. "Are you taller than Barack in heels?" Mizrahi asked.

Wednesday
June 18
McLean, Virginia

Fundraising party for Barack Obama at Hickory Hill, the home of Ethel Kennedy, attended by a number of Kennedys, as well as Megan and Don Beyer; Rachel Goslins, Julius Genachowski; Betsy Katz, Reed Hundt; and Bill Kennard.

$28,500/person

Friday
June 20
Jacksonville, Florida

Fundraiser at the Prime F. Osborn III Convention Center

$500-2,300/person

Monday
June 23
Albuquerque, New Mexico

"Change that Works for You" discussion with working women at the Flying Star Café. Obama speaks to roughly 35 female employees of the Flying Star Cafe chain.

Per Kate Nash of Santa Fe's
The New Mexican:

"Obama, who has been able
to draw crowds around the
country of thousands, seemed
focused on getting votes
one at a time during
the intimate, invited-only
event. His voice at times
was absorbed by the giant
bags of coffee beans from
countries including
Guatemala and Brazil, which
were stacked on shelves
almost halfway to the
ceiling. "

Tuesday
June 24
Los Angeles, California

Fundraising dinner at the Dorothy Chandler Pavilion for over 200 high-dollar contributors, with donations ranging in amounts from $28,500 to $50,000.

Fundraiser at the Los Angeles Music Center, Dorothy Chandler Pavilion
$2,300/person

Notable: This is the first time Obama returns to Los Angeles since winning the Democratic nomination.

Attendees at the evenings fundraisers included a large number of celebrities, stars, politicos and Hollywood executives, including Samuel L. Jackson, Seal, Heidi Klum, Sidney Poitier, William, Cedric the Entertainer, Don Cheadle, Dennis Quaid, Kal Penn, Ari Emanuel, Ron Meyer, Bryan Lourd, Mike and Irena Medavoy, Jim Wiatt, Sherry Lansing, and former Clinton White House official John B. Emerson.

The combined events are said to have raised more than $5 million.

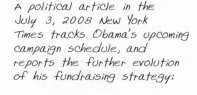

A political article in the July 3, 2008 New York Times tracks Obama's upcoming campaign schedule, and reports the further evolution of his fundraising strategy:

"We have not been able to have much of the senator's time during the primaries so we have had to rely more on the Internet," said Penny Pritzker, the Obama campaign's finance chairwoman. "Now that we have a little bit more access, the senator is able to do events, and we can use him more."

The Obama campaign was initially powered last year in large part by high-dollar donors, but his schedule of traditional fund-raising events fell off this year in the face of a packed campaign schedule. Mr. Obama attended only a handful of fund-raisers, relying instead on contributions over the Internet.

Wednesday
July 2
Colorado Springs, Colorado

Obama appearance at the 5-star Broadmoor Hotel.
$1,000/person

The Obama Menu for the reception consisted primarily of light fare and hors d'oeuvres, including a wide gourmet cheese selection featuring Brie, Stilton, Swiss, Bel Paese, Gouda, Cheddar, Smoked Cheddar, Dill Havarti, and Gourmandise.

Friday
July 4
Butte, Montana

Family picnic with supporters.

Malia Obama Birthday celebration.

The Obamas host a public picnic that also included a 10th birthday celebration for daughter Malia at the University of Montana.

Michelle Obama led the crowd in rounds of "Happy Birthday," and then noted that for Malia having her mom singing into a microphone might not be the best present for a young girl.

"Now, she's thoroughly embarrassed," Michelle joked.

Monday
July 7
Atlanta, Georgia

Fundraiser at private dining location 103 West

103 West
103 W. Paces Ferry Road NW
Atlanta, GA 30305

Says Executive Chef Matt Rainey, of 103 West:

> "It was an honor to cook for a presidential candidate and, in some small way, to be a part of history. Also, so many high profile Atlantans were in attendance, it was wonderful to prepare food for them as well."

103 West
Atlanta, Georgia

Potato Blinis

103 West
Atlanta, Georgia

INGREDIENTS
1 pound riced potatoes
6 Tablespoons cornstarch
3 yolks
3 egg whites, whipped
1-2 cups cream
salt & pepper

Mix riced potatoes, cornstarch, egg yolks, salt and white pepper.

Add heavy cream (warm) 1 cup.

Fold in egg whites (soft peak). Adjust consistency of the blini batter with more cream if necessary.

Spoon 1 to 2 tablepoon sized dollops of batter onto a heated skillet or griddle. Cook in clarified butter until golden brown, then flip over and cook opposite side.

Chef's Note: The potato blinis are usually served with smoked salmon, crème fraiche, capers, red onions, and eggs.

Executive Chef
Matt Rainey,
103 West

RECIPE

Eggplant spread
(kyma melitzanosalata)

103 West
Atlanta, Georgia

INGREDIENTS
4 cup eggplant (grilled, hung and passed)
2 cup red onion, brunois
2 cup ground walnuts
1/2 cup yogurt (Greek style)
2 Tablespoons garlic puree
3/4 cup red wine vinegar
1 1/2 cup evo
Salt and pepper, to taste
1 cup mint, julienned

Score eggplants with fork, season with salt and olive oil, and then place eggplants over hot grill. Be sure to turn eggplants from the stem side every ten minutes until the inner flesh has totally collapsed.

Remove from grill and allow to cool.

When cool, cut each eggplant in half and scoop out all inner flesh with a spoon. Be sure not to rip outer skin and discard clusters of seeds without wasting any pulp.

Pass the eggplant flesh through a food mill. Hang in cheesecloth over night.

Sweat the red onions in olive oil until translucent and season with salt and pepper.

Place the eggplant into a mixing bowl and whisk the remaining ingredients in order as they come, finishing with the evo.

Season to taste with salt, pepper and mint.

Chef's Note: 1/2 case of eggplant yields about 6 cups of grilled, hung and passed eggplant.

Chef's Note: The eggplant spread is usually served with pita chips and lavosh.

Greek Salad
(Kyma Horiatiki salata)

103 West
Atlanta, Georgia

INGREDIENTS
7 ounces of Tomatoes, large diced
6 1/2 ounces Seedless cucumber, large dice
1 1/2 ounces Green bell pepper, sliced and halved
1 ounce Red onion, sliced and quartered
3/4 teaspoon kosher salt
1/2 teaspoon black pepper, freshly ground
2 Tablespoons extra virgin olive oil
3/4 teaspoon red wine vinegar
2 ounces Feta cheese, imported, cut 1/2" thick, triangle

Slice and dice all vegetables.

Place vegetables in a mixing bowl. Season with spices and dress with the virgin olive oil and red wine vinegar.

Place in a serving dish and top with feta. Nine olives (3 varieties) are then used to garnish.

Note: 1 Recipe = 1 large Asian bowl.

103 West
Atlanta, Georgia

103 West
Atlanta, Georgia

Monday
July 7
Atlanta, Georgia

Fundraiser and dinner at the home of Donna and Michael Coles. Michael Coles is the former CEO of Caribou Coffee and a top Clinton fundraiser. 400 people expected.

$2300-$28,500/person (Dinner with Obama is $28,500)

Tuesday
July 8
Rock Creek Park, Washington, DC

Fundraiser at Sharon and Senator John D. Rockefeller IV's (D-WV) mansion

$28,500/person

Michael Powell of the New York Times wrote that the menu at the Rockefeller mansion included a summer tropics salad, filet of beef with a Mustard-Cognac sauce, and a potato nest, along with French and American wines and desserts of Chocolate

JULY

Wednesday
July 9
New York, New York

Fundraiser and reception at the Grand Hyatt

Wednesday
July 9
New York, New York

Private party and dinner hosted by Barbaralee Diamonstein and Carl Spielvogel at their Park Avenue home.

$33,100/person

Thursday
July 10
New York, New York

Women for Obama finance breakfast with Senator Clinton at Hilton Towers

Friday
July 11
Chicago, Illinois

Obama fundraiser at
the Hyatt Regency

Friday
July 11
Chicago, Illinois

Obama Fundraiser at the popular Chicago nightclub, the Park West,
with Jeff Tweedy of the band, Wilco.

Sunday
July 13
Newport Beach, California

Fundraiser at the Balboa Bay Club
$2,300-28,500/person

Obama Menu Lesson: *Do not try to get Obama drunk at a fundraiser; he is not falling for it.*

Many Orange County notables attended the event, including Arianna Huffington and Rep. Linda Sanchez, in what is often considered a Republican stronghold in California. Nonetheless, the event was rumored to have raised over $1.1 million, more than the McCain fundraiser in the same location. Perry Bacon of the Washington Post tells a funny story from the event:

> At the beginning of his remarks, Obama said, "I'm still looking for my mimosa," as many of the several hundred people in this ballroom were holding drinks. (There were small, tall tables, but chairs only in the back and people crowded into the front of my room, fruit and some others snacks were the food)
>
> So someone handed the candidate a Mimosa, which amused him. He had a sip, then put it down, said "I was joking," before declaring himself "more of a Bloody Mary" guy.

Monday
July 14
Cincinnati, Ohio

Duke Energy Convention Center: Obama presents at the 99th Annual NAACP Convention

Sunday-Tuesday
July 20-July 21
Kabul, Afghanistan

Obama eats breakfast with troops at Camp Eggers
Obama meets and lunches with Afghan President Hamid Karzai at the
Residential Palace.

Kuwait

Obama is received in the Dar Salwa residence of the Emir of
Kuwait Sheikh Sabah al-Ahmad al-Jaber al-Sabah, where he discusses
various topics of mutual importance. This meeting is followed by a
royal banquet

Tuesday
July 22
Baghdad, Iraq

U.S. Embassy Compound: Obama eats breakfast with U.S. Army soldiers.

Wednesday
July 23
Israel

King David Hotel: Obama has breakfast with Defense Minister Ehud Barak

Obama has a dinner meeting at the home of Israeli Prime Minister Olmert.

Saturday
July 26
London, England

Former Prime Minister Tony Blair and candidate Obama enjoy a breakfast meeting at the Hyatt Regency London.

Monday
July 28
Arlington, Virginia

Fundraiser at the home of Art and Sela Collins. Art Collins is the President and CEO of Public Private Partnerships, Inc.

Reported Amy Chozick of the Wall Street Journal

About 40 people attended the catered sit-down dinner held in the basement of the Collins's home. Each attendee was expected to raise $114,000.

Obama went straight downstairs and made a few remarks after a brief introduction by Art Collins.

"I want to thank them for cleaning up their basement. It doesn't always look like this," Obama joked. (The "basement" was hardly a typical basement. It was set up with tables and floral centerpieces. Tuxedoed waiters stood at the ready.)

"If you've got a 14 month old, your basement does not always look this way. We're not going to open any doors so stuff can spill out. But we are grateful. Thank you so much."

Monday
July 28
Chicago, Illinois

Palmer House Hotel: "Women for Obama" fund-raising lunch, featuring Michelle Obama and a menu by celebrity chef, sustainable and organic food guru, Alice Waters of Berkeley, California.

Alice Water is a prominent advocate for healthy food in schools, sustainable farming, organic products, and the Slow Food movement. Right about now, her perceived influence begins to grow in the emerging discussion about the food policies of a potential Obama administration

---

Alice Waters' Illinois Menu for Michelle Obama

Grilled Organic Chicken with Herbs à la niçoise

Summer Vegetables

Baked Stuffed Hargrande Apricots with Vanilla Ice Cream

Alice Waters worked with local Chicago-area farmers and individuals to help supply the lunch.

In touch with the issues, Michelle Obama tells the attendees,

"You can't just make a dinner. It's got to be a nutritious dinner, grown with good, fresh, clean food. That takes time. Trust me."

Tuesday
July 29
Washington, DC

Omni Shoreham Hotel: Obama meets with women leaders

Mayflower Hotel: Fundraising reception with the Asian American and Pacific Islander (AAPI) community

Wednesday
July 30
Union City, Missouri

Barbecue at Union City Park

Thursday
July 31
Houston, Texas

Fundraiser at the River Oaks home of Ginni & Richard Mithoff

5:00pm – Reception with Senator Obama followed by Special Dinner with Senator Obama

Reception Sponsor/Reception Guest/Dinner: Write $10,000 or raise $23,000, $2,300, $28,000 per dinner guest

Thursday
July 31
Houston, Texas

Fundraiser at the 21,000 square foot home of Becca Cason Thrash and John Thrash.

Includes time with Obama, a photo together, and dinner.

Dinner was provided by local catering celebrity chef Jackson Hick. His firm Jackson & Co served a menu of appetizers that included empanadas, tempura vegetables, tuna tartare and mini BLT's. It also included seafood martinis (martini glasses filled with crawfish, shrimp & lump crabmeat), sliced beef tenderloin, curried chicken salad with mango chutney and cashews, roasted fennel potato salad, grilled asparagus and tomatoes caprese.

Candidate Obama also requested lime pie, which Jackson & Co. prepared. This is one of the first times when Obama's fondness for pie is officially recognized. It will however not be the last time.

SEAFOOD MARTINIS

INGREDIENTS
2 cups of lump crabmeat (or small scallops)
20 cooked shrimp, small or medium, deveined and shelled
2 Tablespoons of lemon juice
2 Tablespoons of lime juice
1 celery stick, chopped or diced
1 large tomato, diced
1 shot of vodka or cachaca
1 Cup of cilantro, chopped
2 teaspoons of white horseradish
Salt and ground pepper to taste

Mix all ingredients together in a bowl, and allow to marinate in refrigerator for 2-3 hours.

Divide among 4-5 martini glasses, and top with an olive for garnish.

* Recipe courtesy of TasteTV.com

53

Monday
August 4
Boston, MA

Fundraiser at the State Room.
Birthday Celebration.
60 State Street, 33rd Floor
4:00pm – Doors open for Birthday
Celebration with Senator Obama
5:00pm – Doors open for 47th Birthday Dinner and Photoline Reception
with Senator Obama
Celebration Co-Chair/Sponsor/Friend/Ticket Price: $25,000, $4,600,
$2,300, $1,000.
Dinner and Photoline: $28,500 per couple, $15,000 per seat

Wednesday
August 6
Minneapolis, Minnesota

Fundraiser at the Hilton
1001 Marquette Avenue South
4:30pm – Photo Reception with Senator Obama
5:00pm – General Reception with Senator Obama
Dinner/Photo Reception/Ticket Price: $28,500, $5,000, $1,000

Per Pat Doyle of the Star Tribune:

> More than 350 campaign contributors – some of them donating
> $28,500 to dine with a presidential candidate -- cheered
> Democrat Barack Obama Wednesday at an exclusive fundraiser for
> him at the Minneapolis Hilton Hotel.
>
> "I am absolutely convinced we will win Minnesota," the Illinois
> senator said to roaring applause.
>
> 50 people paid $28,500 each to dine privately with the Illinois
> senator. The Obama Menu included lettuce cup salad, beef
> medallions, followed by birthday cake from U.S. Sen. Amy
> Klobuchar (D-Minn) and other Minnesota supporters.

AUGUST

Democratic Party of **Virginia**

HOME | NEWS | THE PARTY | CANDIDATES | ACTION CENTER | CONTACT
PARTY FEATURES ★

Michelle Obama In Norfolk
Posted by Greg on Wednesday, July 30

Please Join

Michelle Obama

and

Tim Kaine and Anne Holton

for an evening benefitting the Obama Victory Fund

with a performance by Bruce Hornsby.

Wednesday, August 6th at 6:00 PM

Harrison Opera House
160 East Virginia Beach Boulevard
Norfolk, Virginia 23510

$10,000 Co-Host (raise/contribute)
$2,500 (includes VIP reception, priority seating, and photograph)
$1,000 (includes photograph and priority seating)
$250 Orchestra Section
$100 per guest
$50 student/military guest with ID

Obama talks with customers at The Copper Dome Restaurant

The Copper Dome Restaurant
1333 Randolph Ave
St Paul, MN 55105

Mahalo, it's Pau Hana Time!

**Obama goes back home to Hawaii
to visit family, friends, and
supporters.**

The Kahala Hotel & Resort
Honolulu, Hawaii

Obama fundraiser at the Kahala Hotel & Resort.

The Kahala Hotel & Resort
5000 Kahala Avenue
Honolulu, Hawaii 96816-5498
www.kahalaresort.com

At the event, pupus, or hors d'oeuvres, were passed around for guests.

Says Kahala Chef Wayne Hirabayashi:

Q. What was it like to cook a meal for the Presidential candidate?

H: It was exciting. It was an honor for my staff and me to represent The Kahala Hotel & Resort.

Q. What is your cooking philosophy?

H. My cooking philosophy is to use fresh seasonal local ingredients, as well as those from around the world. I keep my cooking simple, with the focus on the ingredients and to showcase Hawaii's multiculture cuisines.

Chef Wayne Hirabayashi's Obama Menu

* Roasted Kahuku Eggplant, Waimanalo Tomatoes, and Mozzarella on Pepper Crostini

* Stuffed Mushrooms with Maui Goat Cheese and Sun-dried Tomatoes

* Smoked Huli Huli Chicken with Papaya on Crispy Baguette

* Chinese Roasted Pork with Steamed Rice Flour Buns with Plum and Hoisin Sauces with Julienne Baby Green Shallots

---

The Kahala Hotel & Resort
Honolulu, Hawaii

Assorted Nigiri sushi / Ikura sushi

For the assorted Nigiri sushi
INGREDIENTS
2.10 ounces Assorted seafood – sliced 1ounce slice – length wise
(Tuna Ika, Ebi, Tako, Salmon, Hamachi & Smelt roe)
1.5 ounces Sushi rice – formed into a small ball
.5 ounce Wasabi paste

Slice assorted seafood length wise - approximately 3 inch x 1/2 inch strips

Spread wasabi paste on small rice ball - place sliced seafood on top of rice ball – reform using hands

Present fish side up

For the Ikura sushi
INGREDIENTS
1.5 ounces Sushi rice – formed into a small ball
2 strips Nori cut into 4inch length x 3/4 inch height Nori strip
3 ounces Ikura

Using the same rice balls as for the Nigiri sushi - wrap the 4 x 1/2 inch Nori strip around the rice ball - leaving a open space on top of the rice with the Nori wrapped around - should be at least 1/2 inch above the top of the rice.

Place Ikura on top of the rice & serve

The Kahala Hotel & Resort
Honolulu, Hawaii

RECIPE

Smoked chicken with papaya on crispy baguettes

1 dozen

INGREDIENTS
4 ounces Smoked chicken diced 1/8" (see recipe)
.8 ounces Celery minced
1 1/2 ounces Mayonnaise
.05 ounces Chopped Italian parsley
2 ounces Papaya diced 1/8"
2 ounces Baguettes sliced 1/8" thick
2 ounces Garlic olive oil
1 ounce Butter softened
.8 ounces Lollo rossa
.05 ounces Italian parsley

Toast sour dough bread with garlic and olive oil

Mix together chicken, celery, mayonnaise and parsley

Pipe butter on toast, followed by lollo rossa, the chicken salad, the papaya and then the parsley

Roasted Chinese duck with cilantro and plum sauce

INGREDIENTS
4 ounces Chinese roast duck
2 teaspoons Hoisin sauce
.05 ounces Cilantro chopped fine
.05 ounces Salt
.25 ounces Sugar
2 teaspoons Salad oil
.25 ounces Green onions
2 ounces Baguettes
.05 Garlic minced
2 Tablespoons Olive oil
2 ounces Softened butter
.25 ounces Lollo rosa

Remove the fat from the duck and dice both the fat and the skin

Cut some of the green onions on a bias and reserve it till later, chop the rest of the green onion fine.

Mix the duck, cilantro, Hoisin, salad oil, salt, sugar, and the chopped green onions

Toast baguettes with garlic and olive oil

Pipe butter on each baguette, followed by a piece of lollo rosa, a spoonful of the duck mixture and garnish with the bias cut green onions.

The Kahala Hotel
& Resort
Honolulu, Hawaii

Roasted eggplant and pepper crostini with tomato and mozzarella

INGREDIENTS
4 ounces Eggplant
.08 ounces Garlic minced
.05 ounces Salt
.02 ounces Pepper black fresh cracked
4 ounces Olive oil
2 ounces Wonton chips – cut into quarters & fried
2 ounces Tomatoes
2 ounces Mozzarella
1 ounces Balsamic dressing (see recipe)
1/2 ounce Pesto (see recipe)
1 ounce Butter soft

Toast baguettes with a little of the garlic and a little of the olive oil

Slice the eggplants lengthwise about 1/8" thick and season it with salt, pepper, garlic and olive oil

Broil eggplant to perfection

Slice the tomatoes and the cheese thinly bite size so it can be placed nicely on the wonton chip

Pipe butter on chip followed by the eggplant, the tomatoes, mozzarella, and finally the balsamic and pesto

The Kahala Hotel & Resort
Honolulu, Hawaii

Roasted Kauai prawn with Iberico ham

INGREDIENTS
*4 pieces Kauai prawn – peeled &
deveined*
4 slices Iberico ham

Lightly season the prawns with salt
& fresh grind white pepper, wrap the
Iberico ham around the prawns &
brown on flat grill & finish in pre
heated 350F oven

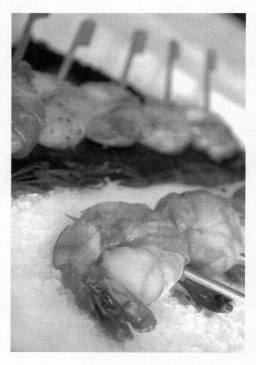

Stuffed mushroom with Maui goat cheese & sun dried tomatoes

4 pieces

INGREDIENTS
4 pieces Medium sized mushroom caps
1 ounce Olive oil
1/2 ounce Chopped fine garlic
1 teaspoon Chopped Italian parsley
2 ounces Maui goat cheese
2 ounces Cream cheese
1 ounce Sun-dried tomato, finely chopped

For mushroom caps – marinate with olive oil, garlic & herbs – roast in a pre heated 350F
oven till tender but firm to the touch – remove from the oven & cool

Combine the goat cheese, cream cheese & sun-dried tomato and mix well

Pipe goat cheese mixture into the mushroom caps & garnish with sun-dried tomato

Chinese Roast Pork with bun

INGREDIENTS
2 ounces Roast pork
1/2 ounce Julienne green onion & red chili
1 teaspoon Hoisin sauce
1 pc Steam bun

For the roast pork – yields 4 portions
2 pounds Pork shoulder
1 Tablespoon Hawaiian rock slat
1/4 teaspoon Five-spice
1/4 teaspoon Dried crushed chili flakes
1/4 teaspoon Ground white pepper
1/4 teaspoon Ground ginger
1 piece Crushed star anise

Steam the bun for 15 seconds – then place sliced roast pork into bun garnish with Hoisin sauce, julienne green onion & red chili & serve

For the roast pork – combine all seasoning together & mix well - season the pork shoulder well & place into vacuum bags – seal & Sous vide at 170F for 6-8 hours or until tender. Remove from bags & pour over hot oil to crisp skin – cut into portions & serve

The Kahala Hotel & Resort
Honolulu, Hawaii

Sunday
August 17
San Francisco, California

Fundraising VIP reception for Asian and Pacific Islanders and dinner at the Fairmont Hotel.

Dinner was for approximately 350 people. In attendance at the events were Craigslist founder Craig Newmark and African-American/Indian-American San Francisco District Attorney Kamala Harris.

The Obama campaign raised $7.8 million this evening.

The Fairmont's Obama Menu included heirloom tomato salad, lavender salt-crusted beef tenderloin and carrot cake cream cheese mousse. $2,300/person (dinner)

According to the San Francisco Chronicle, Obama told a story to the attendees where he said that when he went to Occidental College, his first roommate was Pakistani. In his dorm, he said with a laugh, "Indians and Pakistanis came together under one roof ... to cause havoc in the university."

To applause, he said he became an expert at cooking dal and other ethnic dishes, though "somebody else made the naan," the trademark Indian bread.

AUGUST

LEADING UP TO THE DEMOCRATIC NATIONAL CONVENTION IN DENVER, OBAMA BEGINS A CRISSCROSSED EATING TOUR OF MIDDLE AMERICA (as well as a grass-roots political campaign)

Thursday
August 21
Petersburg, Virginia

Obama stops for lunch at Longstreet's Deli

Sunday
August 24
Eau Claire, Wisconsin

Barbeque at Rod and Gun Park

August 25-28
Democratic National Convention
Denver, Colorado

Obama Menus are rampant at restaurants and bars in Denver during the DNC convention.

AUGUST

DEMOCRATIC PRESIDENTIAL TICKET OBAMA AND BIDEN CONTINUE THEIR CRISSCROSSED EATING TOUR OF MIDDLE AMERICA (as well as their grass-roots political campaign)

Friday
August 29
Aliquippa, Pennsylvania

The Obamas and the Bidens go to the Windmill Ice Cream Shop for ice cream.

Saturday
August 30
Boardman, Ohio

The Obamas and the Bidens go to the Yankee Kitchen Family Restaurant for breakfast

Monday
September 1
Monroe, Michigan

Obama attends the Labor Day barbeque at Plumbers and Pipefitters Local 671

Wednesday
September 3
Dillonvale, Ohio

Obama attends barbeque at the Bergallini family farm.

Wednesday
September 3, 2008

"Dinner with Barack," sponsored by the Obama Campaign

Every supporter who made a donation of $5 or more between July 26th and July 31st took part in our second Dinner with Barack campaign.

On Labor Day, September 3rd, four lucky supporters from all over the country will join Barack for an evening of good food and good conversation.

Meet Barack's Dinner Guests
The table has been set for the second Dinner with Barack.

While a typical political dinner these days consists of officials being wined and dined by Washington lobbyists and bigwigs from special interest PACs, Barack will be sitting down with four regular people from across the country who will share their stories and discuss the issues that matter most to them.

Gabrielle Grossman of Exeter, New Hampshire
Gabrielle worked as a 7th grade teacher but recently became a stay-at-home mom. She's been volunteering for more than a month with the campaign. The day she signed up to volunteer, she found out some tough news: her 2-year-old son was diagnosed with autism.

In her letter to Dinner with Barack, Gabrielle said, "There is not enough funding to get kids the services they need. So many kids are getting diagnosed, and there just aren't enough resources out there for kids. That's a huge issue for me personally."

The campaign has kept her motivated and energized throughout this tough time in her life. She adds, "At a time when you don't feel like you have a lot of hope, it's done the total opposite, the campaign has got us involved and given me more hope than ever."

Brittany Washington of Los Angeles, California
Brittany is a Howard University student who wants to join Teach for America, get her doctorate in education and public policy, and possibly open her own charter school. She currently volunteers in Washington, D.C.'s public school system and says, "The windows are broken out, and there are never enough chairs or lights. It's just ridiculous. And we expect these kids to compete with other kids who have chairs and

windows." Brittany's mother, who used California's welfare medical coverage, recently passed away at the age of 38. Despite Brittany's repeated pleas for a cancer specialist, she was told doctors wouldn't look at her mother because she didn't have the right kind of insurance. She says she admires Barack's style of politics because "it's honest and realistic." As a political science major, she wants to ask him how he's able to work in politics and stay true to his beliefs.

Michael Wilson of Cocoa Beach, Florida
Mike is an Air Force veteran of Operation Iraqi Freedom who disagreed with why we went to Iraq. He plans to talk to Barack about some of the people he met in Iraq -- for example, an Iraqi physician who invited him into his home and wanted to talk about anything except war and politics, and a young Iraqi who dreamed about coming to America. Although Mike is a registered Republican, he believes Barack reflects "what America is and what America needs." And that, he explains, is the place where "people look for freedom and hope. It's not imperialistic; it offers a light." He hopes that Barack will position the country to be that light again.

Dorothy Unruh of Lakewood, Colorado
Dorothy is a senior citizen who is fed up with the current state of our government. As she said in her letter, "I'm sad that our great nation has lost its stature in the eyes of the rest of the world. I have been a registered Republican for years, but recently officially changed parties so I can attend the Democratic caucus and help elect Senator Obama. He is like a breath of fresh air to my husband and me." Dorothy has never taken part in a political campaign before, but she and millions of other voters who want change are going to be the key to Democratic victories up and down the ballot next year

Friday
September 5
Wyoming, Pennsylvania

Obama greets customers at the Avenue Diner

Avenue Diner
22 Wyoming Ave
Wyoming, PA 18644

Friday
September 5
Middletown, New Jersey

Fundraising dinner at the home of musician Jon Bon Jovi

Tuesday
September 9
Abingdon, Virginia

Obama stops for a milkshake and talks with customers at the Ellis Soda Shoppe & Grill

SEPTEMBER

Wednesday
September 10
Washington, DC

Walter E. Washington Convention Center: Attends the Congressional Hispanic Caucus Institute Annual Awards Dinner

Thursday
September 11
New York (Harlem), New York

Lunch with former President Bill Clinton at Clinton's office

Tuesday
September 16
Los Angeles, California

Streisand Sings for Obama in front of Hollywood Supporters.

Fundraising dinner at the Greystone Estate in Beverly Hills, followed by a fundraising reception and concert at the Beverly Wilshire Hotel in Beverly Hills.

Dinner at 5pm for around 250 people at the Greystone Mansion, with tickets at $28,500/person.

**Greystone Mansion
Beverly Hills, CA**

Regent Beverly Wilshire Hotel,
Beverly Wilshire Hotel
9500 Wilshire Boulevard
Beverly Hills, CA 90212

Co-hosts were filmmakers Steven Spielberg, Jeffrey Katzenberg, David Geffen and political networker Andy Spahn. The Mansion was the setting for well-known films such as "Air Force One" and Ghostbusters."

The Obama Menu was reported to include salad with goat cheese, fillet of beef, asparagus and chocolate lava cake.

The Regent Beverly Wilshire hotel event had around 800 people at $2,500/person, and entertainment by Barbra Streisand. Celebrity attendees at both events included Will Ferrell, Jodie Foster, Leonardo DiCaprio, Chris Rock, Pierce Brosnan and Jamie Lee Curtis. Total rasied for Obama was over $8 million.

Thursday
September 18
Bernalillo, New Mexico

Obama gets enchiladas, pie and a cookie while talking to customers at the Range Cafe.

The Range Cafe
925 Camino Del Pueblo
Bernalillo, NM 87004
www.rangecafe.com

Photos courtesy of
the Range Cafe

Thursday
September 18
Albuquerque, New Mexico

Fundraiser at the home of Paul Blanchard, President of the Downs at Albuquerque racetrack.

Friday
September 19
Coral Gables, Florida

Obama Victory Fundraiser,

Country Club Ballroom at the Biltmore Hotel

5:30 PM-8:30 PM

Biltmore Hotel
1200 Anastasia Avenue
Coral Gables, FL 33134

According to Chef Rolando Cruz-Taura, Mr. Obama requested a plain piece of fish with steamed rice. He served 1 Sea Bass and 1 Snapper both with white rice.

Other Hors d'oeuvres are from Chef Rolando's Obama menu below.

Biltmore Hotel Obama Menu

-Idaho Potato Lollipops with Cheddar Cheese, Crispy Bacon & Chive Sour Cream

-Peking Duck Spring Roll with Hoisin BBQ Sauce

-Maine Lobster & Caviar Tartlet

-Spanish Chorizo Empanadas with Huitlacoche Cream

Biltmore Hotel
Coral Gables, Florida

Chorizo Empanadas with Huitlacoche Cream

For the Filling
INGREDIENTS
2 Tablespoons Olive Oil
1 each Small Onion, Finely Diced
3 each Garlic Cloves, Finely Chopped
8 ounces Fresh Ground Chorizo (Not the dry variety)
2 Tablespoons Tomato paste

Heat the oil in a skillet and then sauté the onion and garlic.
Add the chorizo and cook stirring frequently until the meat is broken up and cooked thoroughly.
Add the tomato paste, cook for 3 minutes stirring.
Drain off any excess fat and set aside.

For the Empanada Dough
INGREDIENTS
1 pound, All Purpose Flour
3 Tablespoons Butter or Shortening
1 1/4 Cup Chicken Stock
Peanut Oil for Frying

Warm the stock and the butter or shortening until melted.
Remove from the heat and set aside until cool enough to work with.
Combine the warm liquid with the flour and work it into a smooth paste.
Wrap in plastic and refrigerate for 1 hour.
Divide the dough and working with one piece at a time roll it out to about 1/8" thickness
Cut circles approximately 3" in diameter.
Fill each circle with a spoonful of filling, close into a half moon shape and crimp using the tines of a fork
Using a deep fat fryer or a large pot with a thermometer, heat the oil to 350° F.
Carefully fry each empanada a few at a time until golden brown.
Remove from oil and drain on several paper towels.
Season them with salt and pepper.
Serve with Huilacoche Cream.

For the Huitlaoche Cream
INGREDIENTS
1 can (3 1/2 oz) Huitlacoche (Corn Smut)
1 cup Sour Cream

Whisk the ingredients together and then strain through a fine mesh.
Keep refrigerated until ready to serve

Idaho Potato Lollipops with White Cheddar Cheese, Crispy Bacon, and Chive Sour Cream

Makes about 32 Lollipops

INGREDIENTS
2 Idaho Russet Potatoes
32 Bamboo Skewers
1/4 pound Fresh Chives
1 quart Water
1/4 cup Salt
1 cup Sour Cream
Peanut Oil for Frying
1/2 cup White Cheddar Cheese, grated
1/4 cup Bacon – Cooked and Finely Chopped

Peel the potatoes and then evenly slice them lengthwise 1/2" – 3/4" thick (preferably using an electric slicer or a mandolin).

Using a round cutter (#30, approximately 1 1/2" Diameter) cut out circles from the potato slices and place them in a sauce pan with cold salted water.

Gently bring the potatoes in water to a boil and then simmer until fork tender, careful not to overcook.

Remove the potatoes from the water and submerge them in ice water for a minute, then drain.

Place a single bamboo skewer half way through each potato slice.

Place the lollipops in a single layer in the refrigerator.

Now make the chive sour cream by first bringing a quart of water and a 1/4 cup of salt to a boil.

Have a bowl of ice water readily available.

When the water is boiling, place the chives in the water and boil for 15 seconds, immediately take them out of the boiling water and plunge them in the ice water.

Drain the chives and place them in a clean kitchen towel, squeeze out all excess water.

Place the blanched chives in blender and start the motor, gradually add the sour cream. Pass through a strainer and reserve.

Using a deep fat fryer or a large pot with a thermometer, heat the oil to 350° F.

Carefully fry each lollipop a few at a time until golden brown.

Remove from oil and drain on several paper towels.

Season them with salt and pepper.

Top each lollipop with cheese, bacon and chive sour cream

Peking Duck Spring Rolls with Hoisin Dipping Sauce

About 36 spring rolls

For the Duck
INGREDIENTS
1 Whole Duck, approximately 4 to 5 lbs
2 quarts Water
1/4 cup Grated Ginger
3 each Scallion, cut in half
1/4 cup Honey
2 Tablespoons Sherry Wine Vinegar
1 Tablespoon Arrowroot, dissolved in 3 Tablespoons Water

Clean and pat dry the duck, tie a string around its neck and hang in a cool airy place for up to 4 hours. In warm climates, this should be done in a refrigerator.
Fill a large pot with the remaining ingredients except for the dissolved arrowroot. Bring to a boil.
Whisk in the arrowroot solution.
Place duck on a wire rack or a strainer set over a large bowl.
Spoon the boiling liquid over the duck, collecting the liquid that is gathered in the bowl, returning it to a boil and repeating for approximately 8 minutes
Hang duck again, up to 6 hours.
Preheat oven to 350° F.
Place a large pan with 2" water on the bottom rack of the oven.
Place duck directly on the rack above this pan and roast for 30 minutes.
Turn duck over and roast an additional 30 minutes.
Turn duck breast side up again and roast for an additional 10 minutes.
Carve the duck meat and skin off the bone and set aside.
Chop the meat into a small dice.

For the Spring Rolls
INGREDIENTS
1 package Spring Roll Wrappers, (Frozen)
3 Tablespoons Corn Starch, dissolved in 1/4 cup Water
Peanut Oil for Frying

Assemble the Spring Rolls by taking a spoonful of the duck meat, rolling the wrapper and sealing it with some of the corn starch solution.
Using a deep fat fryer or a large pot with a thermometer, heat the oil to 350° F.
Fry the spring rolls a few at a time until golden brown.
Serve with Hoisin Dipping Sauce (below)

For the Sauce
INGREDIENTS
1 Cup Hoisin Sauce
1/2 Cup Ketchup
1/4 Cup Fermented Black Beans, Chopped
2 Tablespoons Orange Zest
1 Each Juice of 1 Orange
3 Each Garlic Cloves, Chopped
1/4 cup Shallots, Chopped
1 Tablespoon Sambal Olek, (Garlic and Chile Paste)
2 Tablespoons Honey
2 Tablespoons Sherry Wine Vinegar

Whisk together all of the ingredients in a bowl.

Biltmore Hotel
Coral Gables, Florida

Monday
September 22
Chicago, Illinois

Fundraiser at the Standard Club

Standard Club
320 S Plymouth Ct
Chicago, IL 60604
www.stclub.org

Monday
September 22
Chicago, Illinois

"Greeks for Obama" fundraiser at the Powerhouse Restaurant and Bar for the Obama Victory Fund

$28,500/person, approximately 40 attendees

Attended by Endy Zemenides (Executive Director of Greeks for Obama) and State Treasurer Alexi Giannoulias.

Said Giannoulias,

> "I think it says something for the type of person that Barack is that I treat him as a family member. ... There is no more caring, genuine, warm, intelligent, capable leader in this country, and I promise you, I promise you, when Barack Obama is elected president, you will be so proud of your support."

Saturday
September 27
Washington, DC

Walter E. Washington Convention Center: Congressional Black Caucus dinner.

FOR IMMEDIATE RELEASE
September 29th

Senator Barack Obama Receives Phoenix Award at ALC '08 Gala Dinner

Nation's Two Black Governors, California Assembly Speaker and Actress Among Other Awardees

"The Phoenix Award recognizes those who through their efforts and accomplishments have made significant contributions to society, and it symbolizes the immortality of the human spirit and an eternal desire to reach its full potential," said Elsie L. Scott, Ph.D., the Foundation's president and chief executive officer. "Our winners continue to inspire and we proudly honor them."

Sunday
September 28
Detroit, Michigan

Fundraiser at the Detroit Public Library

Friday
October 3
Chicago, Illinois

Suspends campaign for a
romantic 16th Anniversary
dinner with Michelle.

Bought a dozen white roses
for her in Pennsylvania.

Tells flower shop employee,

> "These are beautiful,
> I like the arrangement
> and everything, it
> looks nice."

Dinner at upscale spot
Spiaggia, a Chicago Italian restaurant.

Saturday
October 4
Asheville, North Carolina

Grove Park Inn:

Obama makes a surprise
appearance at the North
Carolina Democratic Party's
Vance-Aycock Dinner.

Monday
October 6
Asheville, North Carolina

Take out lunch at the 12 Bones Smokehouse, where Obama chats with customers. He orders the ribs and corn pudding.

Obama is in town to prepare for his debate on Tuesday, October 7th at Belmont University in Nashville.

12 Bones Smokehouse
5 Riverside Drive
Asheville, North Carolina

Tuesday
October 7
Nashville, Tennessee

Attends a dessert reception fundraiser at Vice President Al Gore's home.

Participates in the Presidential Debate with John McCain at Belmont University.

Thursday
October 9
Georgetown, Ohio

Obama Menu Lesson: *He can make a point on the campaign trail.*

Obama and Governor Ted Strickland visit the Fireside Restaurant.

Obama tells Strickland,

> "This is on me, Governor."

Strickland replies,

> "Well, if it's on you, of course."

Strickland gets a lemon pie. Obama gets a coconut cream pie, plus the "Big O" double-decker cheeseburger. While there, they chat with the customers, who were very surprised to see a Presidential candidate.

Fireside employees tell Obama that the restaurant's owner, William Seip, is a McCain and GOP supporter who never votes for Democrats. Seip confirms this is true.

Obama to Seip:

> "How's business?"

Seip to Obama:

> "Not so good; my customers can't afford to eat out."

Obama to Seip:

> "You might want to try it one time [and vote for a Democrat], because you can't get any worse than we've got now."

Fireside Restaurant
30 Sunset Blvd
Georgetown, OH 45121

Sweet Potato Pie

by Pastry Chef Clemence Gossett of Gourmandise Desserts

*Before preparing the filing, roll out the pie dough and place into your pie pan. Glaze the dough with 1 beaten egg yolk using a pastry brush. Line the dough with parchment paper or muffin liners. Place pie weights (or dried beans) over the paper and bake at 400 until just golden on the outside (about 12 minutes for small pies and 20 minutes for larger ones).

Easy Pie Crust
INGREDIENTS
3 cups flour 1 teaspoon salt
1 teaspoon sugar 1/2 cup + Tablespoon water, very cold
10 ounces butter, very cold and cut into small squares

Place the dry ingredients in a food processor and pulse 4 or 5 times.
Add the butter and pulse just until small pebbles form.
Add the ice water and pulse just until a crumbly dough comes together. If needed, add 1 Tablespoon of water at a time until the dough forms.
Remove from the food processor (carefully) ? and form a flat disc. Wrap ion plastic and refrigerate for 1 hour (or 20 minutes in the freezer).
Roll your dough in a shape 2" larger than your pie pan. Using the rolling pin, pick up and gently lay the dough into the pan. Cut, crimp or use the tines of a fork to create a decorative edge.
Bake blind (with pie weights and no filling) at 350 until golden on the edges, or fill according to your favorite recipe and follow its instructions.

Filling:
INGREDIENTS
4 eggs 2 cups organic sweet potato puree*
1 1/2 cups heavy cream 1/4 cup sugar
3/4 cup brown sugar 1 teaspoon cinnamon
1 teaspoon ginger 1/4 teaspoon orange zest
pinch of salt

Using a large bowl and whisk, beat the eggs with the salt.
Add the remaining ingredients and whisk thoroughly.
Remove the pie weights from your baked pie crust. Pour the filling into the pie tin and bake pie at 375 for 35 minutes (20 minutes for smaller pies), or until the center is 'set'.

*You can boil or roast sweet potato, then peel and puree them, or use a canned variety

Media please credit: Chris Barrett | Powerhouse Pictures

OCTOBER

**Friday
October 10
Pennsylvania**

"Pie-gate"

On stops around Pennsylvania, Obama begins a series of pie-themed anecdotes. With the magic of video, pundits begin counting the number of times he says "pie" during a speech. First, they note that in one speech he says "pie" 13 times in an 86-second period. Then later that day he beats this 'record' by saying "pie" 15 times in 104 seconds.

Here's our version of the transcript from one of these speeches, which actually is based on Obama's Fireside Restaurant pie experience in Ohio with Governor Strickland on October 9th:

Recounts candidate Barack Obama to the crowd:

"We decided to stop at a diner because I was hungry and I
decided I wanted some pie.
Pie.
That's what I wanted.

You make pie?
What kind of pie you make?
Sweet potato pie?
I like sweet potato pie. I'm thinking of having a sweet potato
pie here in Philadelphia. Because I've heard a lot of people
are saying they can make sweet potato pie.
I'll put it up against my mother in laws sweet potato pie.

So anyway, they did not have sweet potato pie in South Ohio.
So I had coconut cream pie. The governor of Ohio he had
lemon meringue pie.
So we ordered our pie and I decide that I'm going to take a
picture with the wait staff, because they all say the owner is
a die-hard Republican. So they want to take a picture with me
so they can give him a hard time.

Just as we were re finished taking the picture and the owner
comes out, with our pie.
So I take my pie. And I say, 'I hear you're a die-hard
Republican sir.'

Then I said to him, 'How's business?'"

Friday
October 10
Philadelphia, Pennsylvania

Photo courtesy of Jon Bon Jovi

Barack Obama Fundraiser Dinner at the Mount Airy home of Comcast exec David L. Cohen.

Rock star, Jon Bon Jovi, performs.

Obama makes other appearances during his trip to Philly. Food is a topic that comes up in regards to his candidacy. According to ABC News Senior White House Correspondent Jake Tappe, the following exchange took place in regards to Obama and eating more of Philly's famous cheese steaks:

Pennsylvania Governor Rendell:

> "People are always asking me, why do I like Barack Obama so much? Since June I've had an answer."

Pennsylvania Governor Rendell:

> "Perhaps the only thing I don't like about him is he's too thin."

Saturday
October 11
Chicago, Illinois

Sheraton Hotel

Obama addresses the National Women's Leadership Issues Conference

Alfred E. Smith Memorial Foundation Dinner

MENU

POACHED LOBSTER TAIL

Lobster Salad

Fine Herb Sauce

Sauvignon Blanc, Kenwood,

California

* * *

ROASTED RACK OF LAMB

Vol au Vent with Seasonal Vegetables

Mushroom and Basil Cream

Sautéed Asparagus

Rosemary Sauce

Cabernet Sauvignon, Markham,

Glass Mountain, California

* * *

CHOCOLATE RASPBERRY CADEAU

Flourless Chocolate Cake

Raspberry Gelee, Chocolate Mousse

Garnished with Fresh Raspberries
Served with Muroise Sauce

Thursday
October 16
New York, New York

Roasts Senator John McCain at the Alfred E. Smith Memorial Foundation Dinner at the Waldorf-Astoria.

Says candidate Barack Obama:

I was thrilled to get this invitation and I feel right at home here because it's often been said that I share the politics of Alfred E. Smith and the ears of Alfred E. Neumann.

But I have to say tonight's venue isn't really what I'm used to. I was originally told we'd be able to move this outdoors to Yankee Stadium, and -- can somebody tell me what happened to the Greek Columns that I requested?

I do love the Waldorf-Astoria, though. You know, I hear that from the doorstep you can see all the way to the Russian tea room. It is an honor to be here with Al Smith. I obviously never knew your great grandfather, but from everything that Senator McCain has told me, the two of them had a great time together before Prohibition. So -- wonderful stories...

Of course, I am especially honored to be here tonight with my distinguished opponent, Senator John McCain. I think it is a tribute to American democracy that with two weeks left in a hard-fought election, the two of us could come together and sit down at the same dinner table without preconditions.

Recently, one of John's top advisers told the "Daily News" that if we keep talking about the economy, McCain's going to lose. So, tonight I'd like to talk about the economy.

Given all that's happened these past few weeks on Wall Street, it feels like an odd time to be dressed up in white tie, but I must say I got a great deal, rented the whole outfit from the treasury department at a very good price.

Sunday
October 19
Fayetteville, North Carolina

Obama stops for chicken, collard greens, slaw, wings and baked beans at Cape Fear BBQ and Chicken, but encounters boos and hisses and general bad behavior from various customers at the restaurant.

One woman yells,

"Socialist, Socialist, Socialist — get out of here."

She later refused to shake Obama's hand, and states she believes he's a

"Closet Muslim."

Several patrons express embarrassment by the poor treatment of a Presidential candidate by their townsfolk.

One comments,

"At least he's not a warmonger."

Cape Fear BBQ & Chicken
523 Grove St Fayetteville, NC

OCTOBER

Accompanied by local Jewish politicians Rep. Robert Wexler and Rep. Debbie Wasserman Schultz, plus former astronaut Sen. Bill Nelson, Obama orders Jewish delicacies during a food stop at the Deli Den.

The decision on what to order was peppered with many suggestions by his companions, and a lot of back and forth banter. An exchange reported by observers is said to have gone like this:

Obama: We're gonna get some whitefish

Wasserman Schultz: You want the whitefish salad? Or the whitefish?

Obama: The whitefish salad.

Wasserman Schultz: You ask for whitefish you get the whole fish.

Obama: I don't need a whole fish (laughs)

Obama: We should probably get a cookie. Oatmeal raisin is a great Jewish tradition (laugh).

Wasserman Schultz: Yes, growing up we had so many of them.

Obama: And one black and white cookie.

Wasserman Schultz: Make it two.

Obama: Two black and white cookies. Now that's a tradition. It's a unity cookie (jokingly).

Wexler: (Get a few black and white cookies for the road)

His final order included potato latkes, nova, a pickle, cream cheese and bagels, whitefish salad, applesauce, black and white cookies, and oatmeal-raisin cookies.

A woman customer shouts to Obama,

"Good luck, honestly. We need you."

**The Deli Den
2889 Stirling Road
Fort Lauderdale, FL 33312**

Tuesday
November 4
United States of
America

**Election Day, Senator Barack
Obama wins the Presidency of
the United States of America by a
substantial margin.**

November
Berkeley, California

Pioneering Chef Alice Waters, a long
time advocate for healthier food in
the home and in schools, sends this
letter to President elect Obama. It
causes a firestorm of debate in food
circles on a number of topics ranging
from appropriateness and arrogance to
relevance and accuracy. People fall on
both sides of the issue. The letter
however succeeds in advancing Waters'
agenda of impressing the need for
food policy on the incoming Obama
Administration.

Dear President Elect and Michelle Obama,

Congratulations on your victory! It is with great pride and pleasure that I write to you, the President Elect of the United States of America.

For the last 40 years, I have been immersed in a grassroots food revolution that I believe will make a tremendous difference to the health, security, and values of all Americans. Local, affordable, nutritious food should be a right for everyone and not just a privilege for a few. At this moment in time, you have a unique opportunity to set the tone for how our nation should feed itself. The purity and wholesomeness of the Obama movement must be accompanied by a parallel effort in food at the most visible and symbolic place in America—The White House.

Knowing how quickly the most important decisions are made after the election, I would like to immediately offer my help and that of my colleagues and friends, Ruth Reichl and Danny Meyer, who were instrumental in the success of Margo Lion's Food and Art Fundraiser in New York City. We would be honored to present ourselves as a small advisory group—a "Kitchen Cabinet" if you will—to help with your selection of a White House chef. A person with integrity and devotion to the ideals of environmentalism, health, and conservation would send a powerful message to our country: that food choices matter. Seasonal, ripe, delicious food grown in the United States would inspire your guests and nourish your family.

Of course, I cannot forget the vision I have had since 1993 of a beautiful vegetable garden on the White House lawn. It would demonstrate to the nation and to the world our priority of stewardship of the land—a true victory garden!

Thank you for your consideration. I would like to ask for a conversation with whomever you think could best advance this idea.

With great admiration and hope,

Alice Waters

Post-election, different lists of Obama Favorite Chicago-area restaurants are released. Various reports on this topic as well as any personal information about Obama illustrate the intense public interest in what and where Obama eats. Chicago tourism advocates are quick to respond to the interest. ChooseChicago.com launches the slogan Experience Presidential Chicago.

The media is not far behind:

ObamaFoodorama.blogspot.com
November 11
Obama Eats Here and Here and Here and

Among the fave "presidential Chicago" restaurants listed at ChoseChicago are Rick Bay Topolobampo (upscale Mexican), MacArthur's (soul food), R.J. Grunts (casual), and Michelle Obama's fave, Sepia (American traditional, local & artisanal; the charred baby octopus, is her favorite appetizer). The AP, which seems to have rapidly gone from being a hard news agency to the online all-Obama version of Us magazine (HUssein magazine?), has been running an amazing series of puff pieces about the Obamas, and adds to the Tourism Board's list with further "resources" for Obamacentric visitors. The AP cites Pizza Capri, Calypso Cafe, and Medici on 57th as long-time Obama family haunts. Interestingly, neither the AP nor Ch0oseChicago mentions Italian Fiesta Pizzeria, another Obama favorite; the owners were recently invited to DC to re-create their thin-crust pizza for an exhibition of inaugural food. What caught our attention in the AP story was the mention of Medici's "Obama Eats Here" t-shirt.

NOVEMBER

Chicago Tribune:
November 23
Tapping into Obama's appeal

Chicago organizations marketing the city are riding Barack
Obama's coattails. Examples:
·The Chicago Convention and Tourism Bureau added a
"Presidential Chicago" page to its Web site the morning after
his election, with suggestions on where to eat, shop, play
and stay, based on Obama's family preferences. Site traffic has
spiked 30 percent since the launch. Last week in China, bureau
chief Tim Roby passed out print copies of the page, translated
into Chinese, to tour operators.
·The Chicago Office of Tourism is doubling to 20 volunteers its
corps of "greeters" who lead tours of the Hyde Park-Kenwood
neighborhood, where the Obamas live. Tours also are offered in
Spanish, French and German.
·The Illinois Bureau of Tourism on Monday added a "President-
elect Obama trail" to its Presidential Trails program.

Chron.com
November 23
Obama slept here
By Associated Press

Interest in Obama sites in Chicago is so strong that
the Chicago Convention and Tourism Bureau's Web site at
www.choosechicago.com now showcases places where the Obamas
eat and shop. They include Topolobampo (upscale Mexican food),
MacArthur's (soul food) and 57th Street Books.
Said Laura Baginski, features editor for the weekly
entertainment magazine Time Out Chicago, "I don't know if
we're quite prepared for the attention we're going to get,"
Baginski said. "I think people are interested in seeing where
he eats, seeing where he gets his hair cut."

Friday
November 21
United States of America

Tanya Bricking Leach for the Associated Press publishes an article entitled:

"Chefs Dream up White House Dinners for Obama"

This article officially unleashes the pent-up demand of the food establishment, foodies, and food writers to begin a torrent of recommendations, musings, policies and creations for the Obama Administration.

The Leach article asked eight chefs to cater a fictional inaugural dinner for the soon-to-be president and his wife. The chefs included Rick Bayless, Charlie Palmer, Rachael Ray, Eric Ripert, Charlie Trotter, Alan Wong, Daniel Young, and Andrew Zimmern. Several of these chefs not only own lauded restaurants, but also have published cookbooks and host food television programs.

Bayless says that at his Obama-favorite Topolobampo restaurant in Chicago, the Obamas usually begin with tortilla soup and guacamole, so he would put both on his Inaugural menu. Bayless would include a green ceviche with Kona kampachi, a premium-farmed yellowtail fish from Kona, Hawaii, as a reference to Obama's native state. Rick's main Inaugural course would echo Obama's mother's roots in the Midwest -- roast rib eye from grass-fed beef served with red chili sauce with corn tamales, a dish similar to ones he knows the Obamas like at Topolobampo

Rachael Ray replied that she would make miniature versions of All-American burgers topped with things like blue cheese and arugula or honey-mustard cream sauce. Rachel would include little Chicago-style hot dogs and deviled eggs. "Casual food makes you smile and puts you at ease," said Ray.

Andrew Zimmern, known for his show on the Travel Channel called "Bizarre Foods," says his Inaugural main course would be roasted baby goat with tortillas and salsa, with sides of braised greens and roasted vegetables. Zimmern says his goal is to source native and sustainable food from across the nation in order to represent the country.

Unfortunately, no one says,

"An assortment of Obama's favorite pies."

Wednesday
December 3
United States

Obama Food-Mania increases.

**Sue Kelly of USA TODAY writes an article entitled,
"Are you ready for The Obama Diet?" In it, she claims that the new diet
in town will be The Obama Diet.**

"What President-elect Barack Obama likes to eat and doesn't
like has become a subject of intense interest, both to
purveyors of foods and those who like to weigh in on their
nutritional merit.

For example, Baby Boomers Cafe in Des Moines, Iowa, reports
that it can't make chocolate chunk cookies fast enough,
according to the Associated Press. The Obama family spent a
lot of time in Des Moines during the campaign and the cafe was
right next door to the candidate's headquarters. The Obamas'
fondness for the cookies soon became well known.

The site SteadyHealth.com takes a look at other foods and
meals our future president prefers. The site says foods he
savors include: chili, Mexican food, almonds, pistachios and
vegetables. Dislikes include mayonnaise, beets, soft drinks and
ice cream. The site praises his hearty-breakfast and six-day-a-
week exercise regimes and calls him a role model for trying to
eat right in an incredibly stressful situation.

As you observe the Obamas in the opening days of the new
administration, you can try to follow their lead in diet and
exercise. Or you can choose your own path"

*This statement is prescient in its accuracy. The fact that Barack Obama
eats well, but also likes traditional American fare, and yet still remains
fit and in shape because of his exercise routine and avoidance of bad
elements like salt, is increasingly described as a role model for the
semi-obese nation over which he will soon preside.*

DECEMBER

Lists upon lists are published about Obama's likes and dislikes when it comes to food. A few examples include:

FOOD BARACK OBAMA LIKES:

Scallops
Tilapia
Cheeseburgers with Dijon mustard
Hawaiian style pizza
Nuts
Trail mix
Granola bars
Vegetables (especially broccoli and spinach)
Dentyne Ice
Handmade milk chocolates from Fran's Chocolates in Seattle
Water
Hawaiian Plate Lunch (scoops of rice, macaroni salad, and a meat dish
like chicken, fish or beef)
Chili
Raisins
Roasted almonds
Chocolate roasted peanut protein bars
Pistachios
Mac 'n cheese
Italian food
Mexican food
Thin rush pizza
Pie (many kinds of pie, including cobbler)

FOOD BARACK OBAMA DISLIKES:

Mayonnaise
Salt and vinegar potato chips
Beets
Asparagus
Soft drinks
Beets (he really doesn't like beets)

In his book "Dreams from My Father," Barack Obama also reveals that he ate grasshopper, dog, and snake as a child while living in Indonesia with his mother. We can only assume that this was an eye-opening experience for him. Note, none of these delicacies are on the "Food Obama Dislikes" list.

Thursday
December 25
Kaneohe Bay, Hawaii

Prior to the January 2009 Presidential Inauguration Ceremony, President-elect Obama goes on a two-week family vacation to his native Hawaii.

President-elect Obama visits Marine Corps base on Christmas Day during the troops and family members' Christmas dinner in the mess hall. Wearing a casual shirt and slacks, Obama talked with troops, gave Holiday greetings and praise, and posed for pictures.

Some choices on the Mess Hall's Holiday Menu included:

Ham
Turkey
Candied sweet potatoes with
marshmallow topping
Mashed potatoes
Corn
Broccoli
Roast beef

Linh Tran, a cook who worked on the military dinner said,

"I voted for him. I like him."

December 26-27
Waikiki, Hawaii

"Shave Ice-gate"

President-elect Obama, on vacation but always followed by reporters and the press pool, succeeds in ditching them to spend quality time with his daughters Malia (10) and Sasha (7). They go to the Sea Life Park marine amusement park.

When reporters finally catch up and engage him in banter at the Koko Marina Paradise Deli, Obama is in the process of ordering lunch. He orders a tuna melt sandwich on 12-grain bread with cheddar and tomato and no mayonnaise.

Obama suggests to reporters who were starving for news that they don't have to write all of this detailed information down. When he arrives at Kokonuts Shave Ice & Snacks he offers some "shave ice" to them.

Obama: "Guys, here's your chance."

Obama: "No? I'm telling you, this is really good."

Obama: "I don't think this is against policy."

Obama: "You want one, I can tell."

Reporters do not take him up on his generous offer, but his kids and friends do.

Obama: (To kids) "How is it? Good?"

December 30-31st
New York

The battle of influence over the President-elect's food policy continues.

In a letter to the New York Times, rebutting various previous comments on the topic, former White House Executive Chef Walter Scheib (1994-2005) comes to the defense of the current White House culinary staff.

He writes:

> ...The presumptions of Ruth Reichl, Alice Waters and Danny Meyer, that the admirable agenda they espouse is not currently the practice in the White House kitchens, are false.
>
> Walter Scheib
>
> Great Falls, Va.

This rebuttal sets off a new chain reaction of debate among foodies, food writers, and food advocates, which continues to rage unabated into Obama's first 100 days as President.

2009

Digestifs

THE OBAMA MENU
IN THE
FIRST 100 DAYS

Monday
January 5
Chicago, Illinois

"Check Please!"-gate

Obama's television appearance in 2001 on Chicago restaurant review program "Check Please!" is revealed by food bloggers, the food press, and "Check Please!" station WTTW. The rumor is that Obama appeared on the popular Chicago restaurant television show, "Check Please," but was so good as a restaurant reviewer that WTTW decided that it wasn't believable and they would not air it.

With the public lusting for all things food and all things Obama, national cable channel CNN discusses it on host CAMPBELL BROWN's news program. Below is an excerpt of the discussion:

BROWN: Interesting there.
Finally, Dana, I know a Chicago station uncovered some old tapes featuring a surprise food critic. Tell us about that.

MILBANK: Well, you remember during Watergate, we had the famous 18-minute gap on the Nixon tapes. Now with Obama, we have an 89-month gap.
A Chicago TV station WTTW has just discovered a lost episode of its show, "Check, Please!" taped in 2001 but never aired with a guest restaurant critic I think you may recognize.

(VIDEO CLIP RUNS FROM "CHECK PLEASE")

BARACK OBAMA (D), pre-PRESIDENT-ELECT: I do have to put in a plug for their peach cobbler, which —

FEMALE REVIEWER: Really?

OBAMA: ... people tend to gobble up pretty good.

FEMALE REVIEWER: See if I would lay off these corn cakes and set them on the table, maybe I'd have some room for some —

OBAMA: That's the problem. Those Danny cakes, you know, they'll get you early and then you won't have time -- you know, room for the peach cobbler.

(CLIP ENDS FROM "CHECK PLEASE"):

MILBANK: So, Campbell, I think it's a pretty safe bet that the restaurant that he reviewed is called Dixie Kitchen will probably be upping the output of peach cobbler when the show comes out a little later this month.

CAMPBELL BROWN: Is it just me or did he not look 12 years old to you?

MILBANK: And even skinnier.

CAMPBELL BROWN: Yes.

Dana Milbank, thanks very much.

MILBANK: Thanks, Campbell.

The Dixie Kitchen and Bait Shop is in Chicago's Hyde Park neighborhood, on 5225 South Harper Avenue. Needless to say, after this revelation that Obama loves it, the restaurant becomes even more popular. Many comments in the media have been made that Obama has a future as a restaurant critic if the President-gig does not work out.

Wednesday
January 7
Washington, DC

Photo Courtesy of the White House

**Live Presidents
do lunch.**

Four former Presidents lunch with President-elect Barack Obama at the White house. The lunch takes place in the President's private dining room, and is hosted by President George W. Bush.

The lunch guests include former Presidents George H.W. Bush, Bill Clinton and Jimmy Carter. Food for the lunch comes from the White House Navy Mess menu, known for pasta, burgers, steaks, and low-fat or vegetarian dishes.

President George W. Bush's press secretary Dana Perino says: "President Bush was delighted to have the former presidents and President-elect Obama to the White House today for a historic lunch in the Private Dining Room just off of the Oval Office. Each of them expressed their desire for President-elect Obama to have a very successful presidency. During the lunch, they had a wide-ranging discussion on many different issues facing the United States, and they all look forward to remaining in contact in the future."

President-elect Barack Obama press secretary, Robert Gibbs adds: "They had a very constructive conversation. The President-elect was grateful for their counsel and the spirit of bipartisanship they showed in wishing his Administration success in meeting the challenges we all share as Americans. The President and the former Presidents had helpful advice on managing the office as well as thoughts on the critical issues facing the country right now. The President-elect is anxious to stay in touch with all of them in the coming years."

**Friday
January 9
Washington, DC**

Michelle Obama announces that talented Filipina Cristeta Comerford will continue as White House Executive Chef under the Obama Administration. This definitive announcement follows ongoing politicking, suggestions, lobbying and recommendations from foodies, chefs, organic and sustainable food advocates, and others such as Alice Waters.

Observes Ed Levine in his popular food blog, SeriousEats.com:

"Instead of bowing to well-intentioned pressure from Alice Waters, Danny Meyer, and Ruth Reichl in choosing a White House chef, he [President-elect Barack Obama] managed to retain the current Filipino-American White House chef Cristeta Comerford.

Comerford, according to her predecessor Walter Scheib, served lots of organic vegetables at the White House at Laura Bush's behest. Some of the vegetables even came from a White House garden. Scheib apparently pigeonholed Alice Waters at one of the Inauguration benefit dinners to inform her of all this.

Now, to make all the Michael Pollan disciples (and, I have to admit it, me) even happier, the Obamas have brought their former personal chef Sam Kass, who earned his cred at Avec, to assist Comerford in the White House. Kass is according to our sources a serious food activist and slow food supporter."

The politics of food continue...

**Saturday
January 10
Washington, DC**

During lunch with DC Mayor Adrian Fenty, President-elect Barack Obama talks with diners at Ben's Chili Bowl restaurant.

Saturday
January 17
Washington, DC

**Michelle Obama's Birthday.
Obama's celebrate an evening
dinner on January 16th at Todd
Gray's Equinox. Other diners sang
"Happy Birthday."**

The San Francisco Chronicle publishes an article called

"What will the Obamas eat?"

that underlines the heightening excitement about the new Obama Menu:

> [EXCERPT] Bay Area foodies ask: What will the Obamas eat?
> Stacy Finz, San Francisco Chronicle Staff Writer
> [Excerpt] On Tuesday, Barack Obama and his family will take
> up residence in the White House. He's already picked important
> members of his Cabinet: secretary of state, attorney general,
> director of the CIA, defense secretary.
>
> But, in the Bay Area, where food is discussed with the same
> passion as politics, the real hot topic is: What is he going
> to eat?
>
> Everyone from Berkeley restaurateur and slow food guru Alice
> Waters to Gourmet magazine top editor Ruth Reichl has weighed in
> on how the Obamas should eat and who should run their kitchen.
> Waters, founder of Chez Panisse, even sent the president-elect
> a letter, offering her services as well as Reichl's and those
> of New York restaurateur Danny Meyer in choosing a White House
> chef.
>
> Obama politely declined, said Waters, who added demurely, "I
> don't want to go where I'm not wanted."
>
> The Obamas have decided to keep the current chef, Cristeta
> Comerford, who has been part of the White House kitchen
> staff since the Clinton administration, rising to the rank of
> executive chef under Laura Bush. The Obamas, who have two young
> daughters, like the idea that Comerford, the first woman ever
> to head up the kitchen at 1600 Pennsylvania Ave., is also a
> parent. "I appreciate our shared perspective on the importance
> of healthy eating and healthy families," soon-to-be first lady
> Michelle Obama has said.

Sunday
January 18
Washington, DC

Due to his pressing schedule, Obama is not able to attend the Aloha Inaugural Ball held in his honor, and based on themes from his native Hawaii.

Marriott Wardman Park Hotel
Washington, D.C.

The Aloha Inaugural Ball welcomes everyone in town for this historic inauguration to join us at a gala celebration honoring President-elect Barack Obama and the Aloha state of Hawaii where he was born and raised. The Aloha Ball is a truly unique and special inaugural event that will feature the music, food and culture of Hawaii, embracing the Aloha spirit of unity that shaped Barack Obama's core values.

The Aloha Ball will recreate the musical experience of Barack Obama's youth in Hawaii in the 1970s, beginning with traditional Hawaiian music performed by Manu Ikaika and music and dancers from the Halau O 'Aulani and Halau Ho'omau I ka Wai Ola O Hawai'i.

The Aloha Ball will be serving a complete Hawaiian menu of wonderfully delicious main courses, side dishes and snacks that Barack Obama enjoyed while growing up. Fully stocked open bars will be serving drinks, including tropical drinks. And everyone who purchases a ticket will receive a Hawaiian orchid lei, a wreath of flowers presented as a symbol of affection

The Aloha Inaugural Ball will feature Barack Obama's favorite Hawaiian-style food. As a teenager, his favorite meals came from Rainbow Drive Inn on Kapahulu Ave.

From Rainbow Drive Inn:
- Chili (Hawaiian-style)
- Shoyu Chicken
- Macaroni Salad

Hawaiian food:
- Kahlua pig
- Lomi Salmon
- Long rice
- Haupia
- Fresh Pineapple

Obama's favorite snacks:
- Spam Musubi
- Assorted Sushi

Drinks:
- Open Bar

Monday
January 19
Washington, DC

In honor of Obama's Inauguration on Tuesday, the Hilton Washington Hotel in D.C. hosts one of the "official candlelight dinners."

The reported Hilton Obama Menu includes:

New England Lobster Bisque en Croute

Porcini Dusted Petit Fillet, Port Wine Demi, Complimented with Seared Sundried Tomato Scented Escolar Basil Emulsion

Sea Salt Roasted Tri-Color Fingerling Potatoes

Winter Baby Vegetables

Warm Sticky Toffee Pudding with Vanilla Ice Cream

Partial Inauguration Day Schedule

-- Poet Elizabeth Alexander to read a poem she has composed for the occasion.
-- 12:30 pm (1730 GMT) - Obama escorts outgoing President George W. Bush to a departure ceremony.
-- Obama, Biden and their families attend a luncheon in the Statuary Hall of the US Capitol along with about 200 guests. The luncheon menu is inspired by the tastes of president Abraham Lincoln.
-- 2:30 pm (1930 GMT) - The 56th Inaugural Parade travels down Pennsylvania Avenue from the Capitol to the White House with the participation of groups from across the United States.
-- 7:00 pm (0000 GMT) to around midnight (0500 GMT) - official and unofficial inaugural balls across Washington.
The Presidential Inaugural Committee hosts 10 official inaugural balls

In referring to Mr. and Mrs. Obama, Karen Herzog of the Journal Sentinel coins the term, "First Eater." In an Inauguration Day posting, Karen explains,

"The new first eater casts himself as a political centrist, open to a variety of viewpoints....Will the first family embrace their role model status to encourage families to connect around the dinner table and to make healthy food choices? Elected on a promise of change, Obama didn't have a platform for changing the way America eats. But America's first black president - known for his devotion to fitness and regular exercise - undoubtedly will lead by example."

Herzog then goes on to talk with various food writers who state that everything Obama eats will be scrutinized, and the source of that food will as well. There will be a continued push to use fresh vegetables and organic foods, as well as pressure to plant a much higher profile kitchen garden on the White House grounds. These issues echo those presented by Chef Alice Waters in 2008 in her infamous suggestions to the then President-elect.

Tuesday
January 20
Washington, DC

Obama Inauguration Luncheon

President Obama's Inaugural luncheon was created by the Joint Congressional Committee on Inaugural Ceremonies, who decided it will reflect a Lincoln theme, influenced by the Illinois "Land of Lincoln" in which Barack Obama was a Senator. The foods and recipes are modeled after those Lincoln actually knew, and the china is a replica of that selected by former First Lady Mary Todd Lincoln. The china features the American bald eagle standing above the U. S. Coat of Arms, surrounded by a wide border of "solferino," a purple-red hue popular among the fashionable hosts of the day.

As a nod to the large influence of the State of California on the President-elect's policies and success, other culinary elements such as wine are decidedly from the Golden State.

The actual Inaugural menu was designed and executed by Washington DC's Design Cuisine. Their Executive Chef, Kathy Valentine, explains,

> "What we try and do with the menu is take a look at what they liked at that time and bring it to the current century or year. They liked stews. What we did is we modernized it a little bit."

The Joint Congressional Committee on Inaugural Ceremonies also provide an official description and background of the luncheon they created:

> On January 20, after the newly elected President has taken the oath of office and delivered his Inaugural address, he will be escorted to Statuary Hall in the U.S. Capitol for the traditional Inaugural luncheon, hosted by the Joint Congressional Committee on Inaugural Ceremonies (JCCIC). While this tradition dates as far back as 1897, when the Senate Committee on Arrangements gave a luncheon for President McKinley and several other guests at the U.S. Capitol, it did not begin in its current form until 1953. That year, President Dwight D. Eisenhower, Mrs. Eisenhower, and fifty other guests of the JCCIC dined on creamed chicken, baked ham, and potato puffs in the now-restored Old Senate Chamber.

From the mid-nineteenth century to the early twentieth century, Presidents left the Capitol after the Inauguration ceremonies and traveled to the White House for a luncheon prepared by the outgoing President and First Lady. After the luncheon, the President and his party would view the parade from a stand erected in front of the White House on Pennsylvania Avenue.

As the parade grew larger over the years, and lasted later and later into the afternoon, organizers began to look for ways to hasten its start. In 1897, they proposed that the President go directly from the Capitol to the reviewing stand, and have lunch there, if he desired. Instead, the Presidential party dined in the Capitol as guests of the Senate Committee on Arrangements. In 1901, the President again took his lunch at the Capitol, and the parade delays continued. In 1905, the luncheon returned to the White House, again in the hopes that the parade could start earlier. Eventually, the organizers turned their focus to shortening the parade, rather than the luncheon.

As the twentieth century progressed, the White House luncheons became more and more elaborate. In 1945, President and Mrs. Roosevelt played host to over two thousand guests in what would be the last White House post-inaugural luncheon. In 1949, Secretary of the Senate Leslie Biffle hosted a small lunch for President Truman in his Capitol reception room. They dined on South Carolina turkey, Smithfield Ham, potato salad, and pumpkin pie. And in 1953, the JCCIC began its current tradition of hosting a luncheon for the President, Vice President and their spouses, Senate leaders, the JCCIC members, and other invited guests.

Since then, the JCCIC has organized a luncheon celebration at eight Presidential Inaugurations. Often featuring cuisine reflecting the home states of the new President and Vice President, as well as the theme of the Inauguration, the luncheon program includes speeches, gift presentations from the JCCIC, and toasts to the new administration.

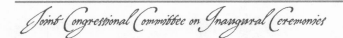 

Joint Congressional Committee on Inaugural Ceremonies

Recipes

Visit http://inaugural.senate.gov

Recipes from the 2009 Inaugural Luncheon

First Course

Seafood Stew

Yield: 10 servings

Ingredients

- 6 (1 Lb) Maine lobsters
- 20 medium size Sea scallops
- 36 Large shrimp, peel, cleaned and tail removed, aprox. 2 lbs.
- 10 (1 oz) pieces of black cod
- ½ cup small dice carrots
- ½ cup small dice celery
- ½ cup small dice leek
- ½ cup small dice Idaho potato
- 1 teaspoon kosher salt
- 1 teaspoon ground white pepper or black pepper
- ¼ teaspoon ground nutmeg
- 1 quart heavy cream
- 1 cup dry vermouth (can be made without)
- 10 (5 inch) puff pastry rounds

Equipment

- 10 (3 ½ inch) terrines/ramekins or serving dish of your choice

Directions

1. Bring 1 gallon of water to a boil; poach lobsters, then shrimp, then black cod and last scallops. After seafood is cooked, remove from water; reserve water and bring to boil.

2. Cook all vegetables in liquid that was used for the seafood, remove vegetables when tender. Allow the liquid to continue to boil until only 1qt of liquid remains. This will be the base for the sauce.

3. Bring seafood liquid back to a boil and add the vermouth and heavy cream and reduce by half, season with salt, white pepper and nutmeg to taste. You have reached your desired thickness when the sauce will cover the back of a wooden spoon. Set aside to cool.

4. Cut Maine lobster, shrimp and scallops into bite size pieces.

5. Pre-heat oven at 400 degrees.

6. Fold seafood and vegetables into cool sauce, being careful not to mix too much as this will break up the seafood. Scoop mixture into terrines or oven proof baking dish of your choice.

7. Cover terrines with puff pastry rounds, brush them with egg wash and bake them until golden brown about 8-10 minutes, allow to cool for 5 minutes before serving. You can cook this 2-3 hours ahead of time and keep warm at 150 F degrees.

*All seafood can be substituted with other favorite options of your choice and availability.

Second Course

Duck Breast with Cherry Chutney

Yield: 10 servings

Ingredients

- 1 tablespoon extra-virgin olive oil
- ½ cup chopped onion (1 small)
- 3 garlic cloves, crushed
- 1 tablespoon finely chopped shallot
- ½ teaspoon black pepper
- ½ teaspoon ground cumin
- Scant ¼ teaspoon dried hot red pepper flakes
- ¾ teaspoon salt
- ½ cup coarsely chopped red bell pepper (½ medium)

RECIPE

- ❧ 1 plum tomato, coarsely chopped

- ❧ ¼ cup dry red wine

- ❧ 1 ½ to 2 tablespoons cider vinegar

- ❧ 2 tablespoons sugar

- ❧ ½ teaspoon Dijon mustard

- ❧ 1 can (3 cups) Bing cherries, quartered *Oregon brand

- ❧ ½ cup Golden Raisins

- ❧ 10 (6 oz.) boneless duck breasts with skin

- ❧ 2 tablespoons water

- ❧ 1 tablespoon chopped fresh tarragon or chives

Method for chutney and glaze

- ❧ Heat oil in a 2 to 3 quart heavy saucepan over moderate heat until hot but not smoking, then cook onion, garlic, and shallot, stirring occasionally, until golden, about 7 minutes. Add tomato paste, black pepper, cumin, hot pepper flakes, and 1/4 teaspoon salt and cook, stirring, 30 seconds. Reduce heat to medium and add bell pepper and cook, stirring occasionally, until softened, about 5 minutes. Stir in wine, vinegar (to taste), and sugar and simmer approx 5 minutes. Stir in mustard, 1 1/2 cups cherries, and remaining 1/2 teaspoon salt and simmer 1 minute. Allow to cool slightly and reserve all but ¼ cup of the mix to the side. Place1/4 cup mix in a blender and puree until very smooth, about 1 minute (use caution when blending hot liquids). Reserve for glazing duck. To finish the chutney, add the remaining 1 ½ cups of cherries, tarragon, chives and all the golden raisins. Can be prepared one day ahead.

- ❧ Put oven rack in middle position and preheat oven to 450°F. Score duck skin in a crosshatch pattern with a small sharp knife and season duck all over with salt and pepper.

- ❧ Heat water in an ovenproof 12-inch heavy skillet over low heat until hot, then add duck, skin side down. Cook duck, uncovered, over low heat, without turning, until most of fat is rendered(melted) and skin is golden brown, about 25 minutes.

- ❧ Transfer duck to a plate and discard all but 1 tablespoon fat from skillet. Brush duck all over with cherry glaze and return to skillet, skin side up.

- ❧ Roast duck in oven until thermometer registers 135°F, about 8 minutes for medium-rare. Remove from oven and allow to rest for 5 minutes.

- ❧ Holding a sharp knife at a 45-degree angle, cut duck into slices. Serve with cherry chutney and molasses whipped sweet potato.

2009 Inaugural Luncheon Recipes

Herb Roasted Pheasant with Wild Rice Stuffing

Yield: 10 portions

Ingredients

- 10 Pheasant breast, boneless, remove tenders and reserve for stuffing, cut small pocket in side of breast for stuffing
- ½ cup Olive oil with chopped rosemary, thyme and sage
- 1 lb. Wild rice, long grain
- 2 quarts Chicken stock or canned chicken broth
- 2 Carrots, diced
- ½ Onion, diced
- ½ cup Dried apricot, small diced
- 1 Tablespoon Salt and pepper mix
- 2 Tablespoons Garlic, roasted

Directions

1. Boil the rice with the chicken stock, cook until soft and most of the liquid is gone.

2. Add the onion, carrot, garlic and apricot. Cook until the vegetables are soft and all liquid has been absorbed. Refrigerate rice mixture until cold.

3. In a food processor, puree pheasant tenders to a paste consistency to use as a binder for rice mix.

4. When rice is cool, add the pheasant puree to the rice until well mixed. Adjust seasoning with salt and pepper and return to refrigerator until ready to stuff.

5. Preheat oven to 400 degrees F.

6. Make 10 small football shaped patties of the rice mix, stuff inside the pheasant, being careful not to overstuff the pheasant. Rub herb/oil mixture on top and bottom of the pheasant, season with salt and pepper. Place the pheasant on a heavy gauge roasting pan and then in a preheated oven for approximately 8-10 minutes. Remove from oven and cover with lid or foil and allow to rest for 10 minutes. Serve over sauté of spinach.

*Pheasant can be substituted with chicken.

RECIPE

Tuesday
January 20
Washington, DC

In an interview in the Washington Post, Washington Convention Center Executive Chef Greg Sharpe confirms he has to prepare a meal for 42,000 ball-goers when Barack Obama hosts six of his 10 official inaugural balls there.

Reports the Post,

> "The menu this year features Italian chicken Roulade (chicken breast stuffed with roasted artichokes, peppers and pine nuts), and two pastas, including a tortellini with a roasted organic tomato cream sauce. Just today, Sharpe's staff made 900 gallons of the sauce."

The Post goes on to provide statistics that underscore Sharpe's challenge. He needs::

8,750 pounds of tortellini
8,250 pounds of Italian chicken roulade
6,000 pounds of penne pasta
1,000 pounds of carrot sticks
150,000 beverage napkins
10,000 bottles of wine
130,000 pounds of ice bagged

The [Official] Inaugural Balls

-- 7:00 pm (0000 GMT) to around midnight (0500 GMT) - official and unofficial inaugural balls across Washington.
The Presidential Inaugural Committee hosts 10 official inaugural balls.

1. The first-ever Neighborhood Inaugural Ball, open to Washington residents and the general public. Using interactive technology, the inauguration team will link this ball with other community balls across the nation. Washington Convention Center.
2. Commander-in-Chief's Inaugural Ball in honor of US active duty and reserve military. Purple Heart recipients, families of military killed in combat and spouses of deployed military. National Building Museum.
3. Youth Inaugural Ball for ages 18 to 35. Washington Hilton.
4. Obama Home States Inaugural Ball with guests invited by Obama's home states of Illinois and Hawaii. Washington Convention Center.
5. Biden Home States Inaugural Ball for guests invited by Delaware and Pennsylvania. Washington Convention Center

Midwest Inaugural Ball, photo courtesy of "Cliff" Carl Clifford

6.   Eastern Inaugural Ball for guests invited by Connecticut, Maine, Massachusetts, New Hampshire, Rhode Island, Vermont, Puerto Rico and the US Virgin Islands. Union Station.

7.   Mid-Atlantic Inaugural Ball for guests invited by Maryland, Virginia, New York, New Jersey, Wyoming, Washington, DC and Democrats Abroad. Washington Convention Center.

8.   Midwest Inaugural Ball for guests invited by Kansas, Indiana, Iowa, Michigan, Minnesota, North Dakota, Nebraska, Ohio, South Dakota, Wisconsin and Missouri. Washington Convention Center.

9.   Southern Inaugural Ball for guests invited by Alabama, Arkansas, Florida, Georgia, Kentucky, Louisiana, Mississippi, North Carolina, South Carolina, Tennessee and Texas. National Guard Armory.

10. Western Inaugural Ball for guests invited by Alaska, Arizona, California, Colorado, Idaho, Montana, Nevada, New Mexico, Oklahoma, Oregon, Washington, Wyoming, Utah, Guam and American Samoa. Washington Convention Center.

The President introduces the new First Lady at the Midwest Ball by saying that he would "like to dance with the one who brung me, and who does everything I do except ... in high heels." Their last dance of the night was at the Eastern Ball.

Sunday
February 22
Washington, DC

National Governors Association Dinner:

The Obamas host their first formal White House dinner. Before they do, Michele Obama takes the opportunity to share the experience with culinary students and the public.

Appetizer: Chesapeake Crab Agnolottis with Roasted Sunchokes
Wine pairing: Spottswoode Sauvignon Blanc 2007 (California)
Entree: Wagyu Beef and Nantucket Scallops
Sides: Glazed Red Carrots, Portobello Mushroom and Creamed Spinach
Wine pairing: Archery Summit Pinot Noir "Estate" 2004 (Oregon)
Salad: Winter Citrus Salad with Pistachios and Lemon Honey Vinaigrette
Dessert: Huckleberry Cobbler with Caramel Ice Cream
Wine pairing: Black Star Farms "A Capella" Riesling Ice Wine 2007 (Michigan)

Discussion with the First Lady, Desiree Rogers, Cris
Comerford, Bill Yosses, and Students from L'academie
de Cuisine
THE WHITE HOUSE

Office of the First Lady

For Immediate Release

**DISCUSSION WITH THE FIRST LADY,
SOCIAL SECRETARY DESIREE ROGERS,
EXECUTIVE CHEF CHRIS COMERFORD,
PASTRY CHEF BILL YOSSES
AND STUDENTS FROM L'ACADEMIE DE CUISINE**
White House Kitchen

3:58 P.M. EST

MS. ROGERS: We are so excited to have all of you here. And welcome to the White House Kitchen. I don't know that you've ever been in here. And so we're delighted to have all the students here. We're delighted to have the First Lady here on the eve of our inaugural dinner. One of the things that you may not know --

MRS. OBAMA: Our State Dinner.

MS. ROGERS: I'm sorry, our State Dinner.

MRS. OBAMA: We did that. (Laughter.)

MS. ROGERS: Our State Dinner.

MRS. OBAMA: Our Governors' Ball Dinner.

MS. ROGERS: Our Governors' Ball Dinner. So we've got representatives from most of the states that are going to be here tonight. And what you may not know is how much planning goes into a meal, and -- from the linens to the flowers. One of the things that -- you know, certainly any meal in the White House is historical, but this being the first State Dinner for President Obama and Mrs. Obama is particularly important for us.

So we've tried to celebrate not only democracy, but really try to intertwine many of the Presidents, through the selections of their china. So for one of the first times, we've mixed china. In addition to that, you'll hear more about the menu. You'll see that the chefs have selected many of the vegetables and the meats from across the country, as well as the wines. And so we are really excited about what is going to occur tonight, and particularly excited that the culinary students are here to really be able to share and interface with the staff here. Maybe one day you guys might wind up being a White House Chef. (Laughter.)

And so we've got 130 people coming tonight to eat in the State Room. And then the President and Mrs. Obama will invite them to hear the Marine Corps Band. And then of course one of the American legends, a band I really love, Earth Wind and Fire, is going to be here. (Laughter.) So with no further adieu, Mrs. Obama.

MRS. OBAMA: Thank you, Desiree. Well, welcome everybody. This is an exciting day for me, for all of us. It's my first official dinner, and I've got with me Cris Comerford, the Executive Chef, as well as Bill Yosses, who is the head of our pastry division. This is so exciting, and I want to just welcome all of the students from L'Academie de Cuisine. You guys are the top students, so we are so excited to have you here. This is going to be a fun day for us. We're going to have good food, we're going to have good music, so we're very excited.

But I am also very excited about the food here at the White House, because one of the things that I was most excited about when I came in was to find that there are so many great

professionals here. This is where the magic happens. No
one would expect that all that comes out of these dinners
happens in this little bitty space, but we have some of the
best talent here.

And one of the things that we wanted to do during our time
in the White House is to showcase some of this talent. And
that's why we have Cris and Bill here, as well, as you can
see, the rest of the crew working away to make this evening
just fabulous.

I can tell you firsthand that this meal is going to be awesome,
because I had an opportunity to do some tasting, along with
Desiree and my mom. We had a wonderful tasting luncheon, and
it was very hard to choose from so many great selections. But

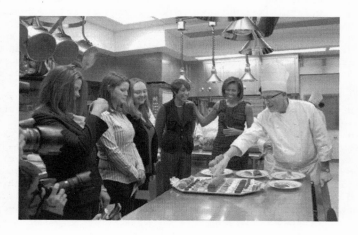

we're going to have just a very good meal.

So with that, I'm going to turn it over to Cris, who's going
to talk a little bit about the menu, and then Bill will talk
about the desserts. And again, you guys, welcome. We hope
to have you back again. And feel free to ask any questions
that you'd like.

Cris, take it away.

MS. COMERFORD: Thank you, Mrs. Obama. First of all,
I want to welcome all of these students in our very big
kitchen. (Laughter.) As you can see, like with any menu
planning, there's a meticulous planning that takes place before
even a Governors' Dinner takes place. And when we did
our brainstorming like a couple weeks back, we took into
consideration a lot of things.

And of course the first things we considered are what's seasonal
and what is fresh, and of course representing the best of

the American spirit. And you have to make sure -- like we tried to look at the northeastern part and see what's the best thing that they could offer at the season. And let me just go through each courses, so every course will be explained well to you.

Our first course is Chesapeake crab agnolottis, which are stuffed pasta with sunchoke puree. I heard a question earlier from one of the press. They wanted to know what sunchokes is. A sunchoke is also called Jerusalem artichokes, but they're not really artichokes; they're actually a root that's very reminiscent of potato and — (inaudible). So it has a very -- ooh, wow, on cue -- (laughter) -- this is Tafari right here, who is one of my assistant chefs, who did just a wonderful plate that we'll be serving tonight. These are three agnolottis that are served with the sunchoke puree, a little basil oil. It's really wonderful. It's very light and airy, and of course it's Mrs. Obama's favorite. So thank you, Tafari.

And then next I'm going to talk about our main course, which is the Wagyu beef, or the -- it's actually an American-style Kobe beef. It's actually a cross-breed of the Kobe and the Angus beef, and actually this particular cattle herd is from central Nebraska. In these particular feed lots, we would, like, feed the beef like grass feeding; 90 percent of it's live, and towards the last 10 percent, it's given nice, organic whole grains, and some -- you know, just to enhance -- you know, fattening and marbling of the meat.

So as Tommy is putting together a wonderful beef on the side, I'm going to explain to you some of these wonderful carrots. I'm going to take it away from Franky, who's actually a graduate of your school. So we have one of your alumni. (Laughter.)

This is a Red Dragon carrots that is growing in a greenhouse in Huron, Ohio. So pretty much, as you can see, what connects all of our menu is really trying to use up things that are indicative of this area, but then at the same time, you know, not forgetting that we could get some things that are good -- let's say, for example, in Nebraska -- just like what the beef represents. So we try to be really very good with using the best of the local products.

And as you can see, what the guys are doing right now is just cleaning it off. And later on, this kitchen at about, like, 5:00 p.m. -- when this press review is over, it's going to be so busy, trying to put together things. Everything is pretty much prepared and done here.

And this is Tommy, my Executive Sous Chef, who put together this wonderful main course. And it's of course the Wagyu beef that's served on a carrot puree. And of course we have some Nantucket sea scallops that are wonderful -- and it's also Mrs.

Obama's favorite, so we have to put it in there.

MRS. OBAMA: The President loves scallops, too.

MS. COMERFORD: He loves scallops, too. We won't forget him, either.

MRS. OBAMA: Don't forget about him. (Laughter.)

MS. COMERFORD: And then for the salad tonight, I mean, you want something that's really light and very citrusy, to kind of like finish this course. It's not, you know, technically heavy, but it's really kind of like -- thank you, Sam. Sam here has put together a wonderful plate of -- you want to explain what's on this?

MR. KASS: Sure. So these are -- we'll start from the bottom up. On the bottom is watermelon radishes that are grown very close to here. They're really big and beautiful. And it's a citrus salad, so we carve our oranges and grapefruit. And then our lettuces are mixed with ice plants, which grow really well through the winter. And we have crystal lettuce, and they're very -- basically the same variety of plant, and with Sicilian pistachios that have been lightly candied, and a honey citrus vinaigrette. So it should be very tasty.

MS. COMERFORD: Thank you, Sam.

MR. KASS: You're welcome.

MS. COMERFORD: And of course you saw all of the three courses. And of course this course won't mean anything without Bill explaining -- (laughter) -- the dessert. So I'll pass it on to you.

MR. YOSSES: Thank you. Thanks. The desserts are in the same philosophy as the main courses, in that we like to use regional specialties, natural and unadulterated, whenever possible. So tonight we're going to be serving a huckleberry cobbler with caramel ice cream. It's one of the First Family's favorites.

And here's the huckleberries. They come from Idaho, so I sort of have the West Coast covered. (Laughter.) Idaho and Washington state, Oregon, they all specialize in huckleberries. As you may know, it's a wild product, it's a wild bush that grows on the mountains. They have not been able to cultivate it yet, though they tried. Mother Nature seems to want to keep those for herself.

So we are proud to serve this tonight, and happy to have you with us.

MRS. OBAMA: And we're going to have ice cream, right?

MR. YOSSES: And ice cream, as well. (Laughter.) You've got to have that, yes.

MRS. OBAMA: Homemade.

MR. YOSSES: Let me -- in the meantime, I can bring some of these pieces.

For the after-dinner guests, we don't want to forget them, so we brought a little selection of goodies for them, as well. These are maple truffles; New Orleans pralines -- they seem to be requested quite often -- (laughter); a pear layer cake; these are cheesecake lollipops; this is a huckleberry -- a little version of the huckleberry tart for the after-dinner guests; a meringue; and a raspberry tart; and a passion fruit.

So we're going to bring you some samples, and everybody can try them out.

MRS. OBAMA: Questions? Are there any questions?

Let me just say before we open it up, I just want to reiterate just how professional and gracious this staff has been. I mean, one of the delights of living here is working with everyone here who has just gone above and beyond to make this place feel like a home -- everything from Bill, you know, helping the kids make desserts with friends, to Tommy and the guys making french fries whenever you want. They can do this, but they can also make a mean batch of french fries -- (laughter) -- when you want it done.

And one of the things we want to highlight, we want the world to know, is that we've got this kind of talent base here; people who are committed not just to our family but to this country, and making the White House not just a home but a place of pride and grace for the nation to see it, for the world to see. And I am so grateful to Cris and to Bill and to the entire staff for all that they've done. This dinner is going to be phenomenal, but what makes it special is that every day it feels like home. So I want to thank them, as well.

So, you guys, any questions that you have. Feel free.

Q   Yes, could I ask one?

MRS. OBAMA: Of the students. It's the students' turn. (Laughter.) So jump in. You'll see you'll get left in the dust -- (laughter) -- if you don't ask a question. (Laughter.)

Q   Mrs. Obama, what is the typical size of the staff here? And does that vary, depending on the size of the event that is going on in the house?

MRS. OBAMA: Well, Cris, you probably have a better sense. There's the working staff in the kitchen, which, you know -- what's the --

MS. COMERFORD: It's about seven people, working staff, in the kitchen. We have two full-time pastry chefs. And of course during an event like this, we have a good support staff of like chefs from around here, from the Navy Mess, people that we've worked with before that are reputable; talented and really good.

MRS. OBAMA: So we do a bit of supplementing when it comes to the big events, but not all those people feed us every day. (Laughter.)

Q   A lot of french fries.

MRS. OBAMA: Right, right. (Laughter.)

Q   After the menus have been planned, how long -- how many days ahead do you start to really prepare everything to put together? How long does it take?

MS. COMERFORD: Pretty much, like, to prepare something, we actually -- it takes only two days. But the planning stage is the longest stage, and of course connecting with the growers, with our purveyors, and with our farmers, because for any menu to be successful, those are the key relationships that you have to build. So pretty much this whole menu is built on American relationships. It's very, very important.

MRS. OBAMA: And also, Cris and Bill are very flexible, because they set up a menu, we do the tasting, and we said, oh, we like this with that, and this with the other thing, and we really like the way this tasted. And then they went away and made all our kooky ideas make sense, from a menu perspective. So, you know, it takes a lot of talent to be able to take an ordinary taste -- because what we think is good may not work together in a meal, but they manage to make it work every single time.

Don't be afraid. (Laughter.) You're in the White House. Ask whatever you want.

MR. YOSSES: Now is your chance.

MRS. OBAMA: And these guys have -- you know, even think of the sort of professional questions that you have. You know, how do you -- one of the questions I have is how do you become Executive Chef in the White House?

Q   Are you taking interns? (Laughter.)

Q   I'm looking for a job. (Laughter.)

MS. COMERFORD: Actually, the question about are you taking interns, that would be an Admiral Rochon question. But we do actually -- you know, if there are students who are really good and talented and have the passion to really share your talent with us, I mean we're always open for part-time help in what we call a service-by-agreement. And this is when you get experience in events like this, like a state function, or let's say like, you know, celebrating a picnic outside. So we have a lot of repertoire in terms of representing American cuisines. So any time, if you're interested, just call here.

MR. YOSSES: Especially during the busy months. (Laughter.) Yes, send your resumes, because we're always looking for new people, bringing new ideas. And the students have great ideas, and they're sort of out there; they know what's being talked about and what's being served. So we'd love to hear from you.

Q   And how do you choose your full-time kitchen staff? Are these people you've worked with before, that you brought with you here, or --

MS. COMERFORD: Some people I've worked with before, and once you see a talent, you don't want to let go of it -- (laughter) -- because this -- it's really the team that will make your kitchen successful. And once you build a good kind of team into that you want, they're the backbones. I mean, without their help, I mean, all of this would be just -- it's not going to be executed --

Q   The D.C. restaurant scene has grown and become more well written about. We have a lot of the top-name chefs around in this area, either based here or they have restaurants here. How much do you partner with people like Michel Richard, or other people from the area, to increase the training and the exposure that the staff here have, in terms of the dishes you prepare?

MS. COMERFORD: Well, the thing about the chefs -- (inaudible) -- we have such good relationships with the other chefs in the area, so we kind of like, you know, chit-chat a bit, and we visit their places, and we ask questions, so, you know, trying to take some ideas from them, and share your ideas, too -- and that exchange, I mean, you grow as a chef. I mean, there's no such thing as, like, it's my secret recipe; I'm not going to share this. The best recipe is a recipe that's shared with other chefs.

MR. YOSSES: That's something that you will learn as you go on. And you'll know each other over the years, and some of your best ideas come from that interchange. And we work with -- in the sense that we talk to the chefs in Washington, D.C. And I think the only thing we like better than talking is eating -- (laughter) -- so hopefully we don't do them at the same time. (Laughter.) But we do talk with a lot of the chefs in the area, and exchange ideas.

Q   Do you try to represent different states in most --
in the foods you choose for most menus? Or is just more
specifically --

MS. COMERFORD: It's not necessarily representing a lot of
states, but really representing what the region or area can
cover. So let's say -- I could get, like, the best sunchokes
-- like now, they actually grow in Maine, although they grow
in Arizona, too. But why would I, you know, go to Arizona,
when I could get it closer to me? So, in that way, we reduce
a lot of different aspects of traveling time and shipping.
So that helps.

Q   What's a normal day like in this kitchen? Obviously
you're preparing for a large event today, but just like a
normal, average day in the kitchen?

MS. COMERFORD: A normal, average day, you know, somebody will
open up the kitchen for breakfast and take care of the First
Family, because, you know, between Sasha and Malia going to
school early in the morning, we have to be up there before
they kind of go to the kitchen and sneak in, and make sure
everything is prepared and ready for them.

And then somebody else will come in and take care of what needs
to be taken care of for lunch, because Mrs. Obama likes to
have her lunch a certain way. And we have -- actually have
introduced some dishes that hopefully that she will enjoy for
years to come. (Laughter.)

And then, you know, like -- and then there would be another
sous chef coming in to cook dinner for the First Family also.
And then in between that, we have a support staff that we
have to feed. We have, like, events that we have to contend
with -- menu-writing, purveying, you know, staffing people.
So it's not just the cooking itself. It takes a lot of
different aspects.

MRS. OBAMA: Yes. I mean, the weeks are busy. I mean, it's
not just meals or dinners. I mean, if we have a reception
here, we've got to pass hor d'oeuvres, and the kitchen is
handling that. If we have -- we had 6th and 7th graders
here for a concert, and they all got cookies. Those cookies
were freshly baked cookies. And Bill's shop was on top of
it. And this coming week, we've got a series of things going
on, so -- in addition to them making sure that the family's
needs are met.

And, you know, we're like any other family. Kids have
breakfast, you got lunches, dinners, and we try to maintain a
consistent routine. But then there's everything else that's
going on, on the State Floor, that has to be contended with
that sometimes we don't even realize. You know, we walk down
to the reception, and think, oh, these hor d'oeuvres are really
good, where did this come from? (Laughter.) And Cris was just

upstairs making an omelette. (Laughter.)

Q   Mrs. Obama, what's your -- do you have a favorite thing that, since you've moved in, that the staff here makes?

MRS. OBAMA: That I like? You know, there hasn't been anything that I don't like. There's some mean waffles and grits that are made in the morning -- (laughter) -- that have become a regular staple for some of us. I don't eat waffles every day.

The soups and salads that Cris has made for lunches -- you know, she will come up with some very interesting light, healthy salads. And, you know, being able to make a soup that tastes creamy without being creamy, because that's something that we work on -- it's like how do we keep the calories down, but keep the flavors up -- that's also the important thing about natural or local is that you get things that are really, really fresh.

I think, Cris, you made a broccoli soup the other day.

MS. COMERFORD: It was no cream.

MRS. OBAMA: It was no cream, and I ate it in my office, and one of my staff members was there, and she started scooping. She said, what is this? I said there's no cream in it. She finished it, by the way. (Laughter.)

But, you know, that's one of the things that we're talking a lot about, is that, you know, when you grow something yourself and it's close and it's local, oftentimes it tastes really good. And when you're dealing with kids, for example, you want to get them to try that carrot. Well, if it tastes like a real carrot and it's really sweet, they're going to think that it's a piece of candy. So my kids are more inclined to try different vegetables if they're fresh and local and delicious.

So that's a lot of what I've been impressed with, is just the ability of this kitchen to take some creative things. I think we're also having a spinach tonight that is an amazing spinach. It's a cream spinach without cream. And there is no way you would eat that and not think that it wasn't full of cream and cheese. But it's -- how did you guys make that? I think Tommy may have --

MS. COMERFORD: That's Tommy's creation over there. It's just basically a sauteed spinach with olive oil and shallots. And last minute we -- we just whipped spinach puree, so it gives us a very, very light, airy -- but it's very high in vitamins, because pretty much there's not a lot of cooking done. It's just finishing it so that the vegetables are bright green, so you obtain all of the nutritional value of the spinach and even the flavors.

MRS. OBAMA: It's delicious. Sasha still didn't like it. (Laughter.) That's the other test. It's like I think they have another test, because they're feeding kids, and sometimes kids are like, it's green; that bright green color is horrible looking. (Laughter.) You know, so they have some interesting challenges just meeting the taste issues of a seven- and a ten-year-old, and making food that's healthy and delicious. We thought the creamed spinach would work for them -- (laughter) -- but it's really good.

Q How often do you get shipments of fresh produce in on a weekly basis?

MS. COMERFORD: Of course, it depends on demand. And pretty much of course we feed our support staff here every day, and we do not get delivery, per se, because of security issues. We have purveyors and farmers and growers that we partner with, and pretty much they don't know that it's really coming directly here. But we have local farms from around the Harrisonburg area, in New Jersey, right here in Maryland, in D.C., that kind of work with us to make sure that whatever we get are secure, and at the same time pretty much naturally grown.

Q Just to follow up on the point raised by Mrs. Obama earlier, how did you end up here?

MS. COMERFORD: Ooh. (Laughter.) Just a long story. I don't know, within the context of this press -- (laughter) -- but it's really no such -- I was working at the ANA Hotel as the chef of the fine dining room there. My friend was working in here. I wanted to see what's going on at the White House, but not really thinking that eventually this would be the door that's going to be widely open for me. So I took it. And it was good. (Laughter.)

MR. YOSSES: I had a -- I think it was a small photograph of a dessert in a magazine, and Desiree's predecessor saw it, and they were looking for a Pastry Chef at the time, so she said, would you come down and do a tasting, and, you know, go through that process? And luckily here I am. Yes, I'm very happy to be here.

MRS. OBAMA: The President calls Bill "The Crust Master" -- (laughter) -- because he's a big pie guy, and he has some of the best pies and tarts that come out of this place, and the fillings are just perfection -- which is a problem. (Laughter.)

MR. YOSSES: We have an example of one, if you would like. Speaking of crusts and pies, this is the cobbler from tonight. And students, please begin.

MRS. OBAMA: Eat away.

MR. YOSSES: Don't be shy.

MRS. OBAMA: And as Desiree said, just so that you know, this is the Truman china, and there is a limited number of them, so -- (laughter.)

Q   I believe you said you were intent on using various chinas. But do you have a favorite set of china that you use here, or --

MRS. OBAMA: I haven't gotten to the point where I have a favorite set. I mean, they're all beautiful. This set is -- it's just classic. And it's really appropriate for an important event like this. It makes the table just look luscious, in a way. It doesn't clash with the food, so it's elegant without being too complicated, so you're focused on what the dish looks like, but the plate is still there. So this was a very simple, approachable but elegant pattern. And this will probably be one that we use a lot. But there are so many beautiful patterns to choose from. We're really lucky.

Q   Are you going to come up with your own, as well?

MRS. OBAMA: I think so. I think that's part of the job. (Laughter.) How is it?

Q   Very good.

Q   The crust is beautiful.

MRS. OBAMA: Bill --

Q   Crusty.

MRS. OBAMA: The "Crust Master." And we'll have some for the press. (Laughter.) They're, like, oh. I know, it's not fair, it's right there.

Q   I'm willing to share.

MRS. OBAMA: You guys, come on in. This isn't fair.

MS. ROGERS: One correction. This one is not Truman.

MRS. OBAMA: Oh, no, it's not Truman.

MS. ROGERS: It's Wilson. This plate is Wilson.

MRS. OBAMA: Okay, thank you, everybody. I appreciate it. We appreciate you coming. Enjoy.

END
4:25 P.M. EST

Friday
March 20
Washington DC

First Lady Michelle Obama today breaks ground for the new White House vegetable garden.

This is the Obama Administration's first major food policy decision. It greatly appeals to the growing populist foodie movement, both online and in the kitchens and restaurants of the Nation.

It is hailed as a wise move that sets an example for America and the World.

In a declaration of victory, Celebrity Chef and Sustainable Foods-guru Alice Waters' Chez Panisse Foundation sends out a press release.

For Immediate Release
Chez Panisse Foundation

White House Breaks Ground on Edible Garden
20 years of advocacy pays off for Chef/Author Alice Waters

March 20, 2009, Berkeley, California, First Lady Michelle Obama broke ground on an edible garden at the White House today, culminating 20 years of advocacy by Alice Waters and signaling a national commitment to sustainability and access to fresh, healthy food for all Americans. Especially in these difficult economic times, the garden can serve as inspiration to families everywhere to grow their own food, which can provide a significant cost savings on fresh, healthy produce.

"Fresh, wholesome food is the right of every American," said Waters. "This garden symbolizes the Obamas' commitment to that belief." Waters, who lobbied the Clintons to plant a garden on the White House lawn during their two-term residence, has since launched a school lunch reform effort which she envisions becoming a national program.

About School Lunch Reform
Approximately 56 million children attend public school in the United States, and many of them take their sole daily meal at school. Since 1997, Waters has advocated a change in the National School Lunch Program to ensure that nutritious, fresh meals are available to all children at school.

Waters' Chez Panisse Foundation, in partnership with the Berkeley Unified School District and Chef/Author Ann Cooper, has created a model school lunch program in Berkeley, California, where, within the district budget, ingredients are now fresh, sustainably and often locally produced. Traditional school lunch fare, including highly processed, heat-and-serve meals have been removed. A study by the University of California at Berkeley's Center for Weight and Health indicates that children with high exposure to this program choose healthier food at school and at home.

Michael Pollan noted, "This administration clearly understands the central role that our food system plays in relation to major issues facing our country: health care, energy independence, climate change and local economies. The garden sends a strong message to the country that we will be taking a new look at the food system in the next four years, including reforming the National School Lunch Program."

Waters added, "The choices we make about food impact our health and the health of our communities and the environment. By planting this garden, the Obamas have brought food into the national agenda.

**Thursday
April 9
Washington, DC**

President Obama hosts a traditional Seder dinner in the Old Family Dining Room of the White House. Some friends and White House employees and their families joined the Obama family. Official White House photo by Pete Souza)

No Cream Creamed Spinach

White House Executive Chef
Cris Comerford

INGREDIENTS:
2 pounds baby spinach, washed and cleaned
2 tablespoons olive oil
4 shallots, minced
2 garlic cloves, minced
Salt and freshly ground pepper

Method:

1. Blanch half a pound of spinach in salted, boiling water. Immediately, "shock" the blanched spinach in a bowl of iced water. Drain and squeeze out the excess water. Puree in a blender. Set aside.

2. In a large skillet, sweat the shallots and garlic until translucent. Add the rest of the spinach leaves. Toss and sauté until wilted. Fold in the spinach puree.

Season with salt and pepper.

Serves 6.

May
United States of America

First Lady Michelle Obama joins Elmo of Sesame Street fame to promote healthy eating and exercise -- the basic ingredients of the Obama Menu.

FIN

(until tomorrow's menu)